Samuel Cooper

The first Principles of civil and ecclesiastical Government

Delineated in Letters to Dr. Priestley, occasioned by his to Mr. Burke.

Samuel Cooper

The first Principles of civil and ecclesiastical Government
Delineated in Letters to Dr. Priestley, occasioned by his to Mr. Burke.

ISBN/EAN: 9783337109790

Printed in Europe, USA, Canada, Australia, Japan

Cover: Foto ©ninafisch / pixelio.de

More available books at **www.hansebooks.com**

THE
FIRST PRINCIPLES

O F

CIVIL and ECCLESIASTICAL

GOVERNMENT,

DELINEATED,

(IN TWO PARTS,)

I N

LETTERS

T O

Dr. PRIESTLEY,

OCCASIONED BY HIS TO

Mr. BURKE.

By SAMUEL COOPER, D. D.
MINISTER OF GREAT YARMOUTH.

————Οὐκ ἄρα, ὦ βέλτιστε, πάνυ ἡμῖν ἄτω Φροντιστέον ὅ, τι ἐρᾶσιν οἱ πολλοὶ ἡμᾶς, ἀλλ᾽ ὅ, τι ὁ ἐπαΐων περί των δικαίων καὶ ἀδίκων, ὁ εἷς, καὶ αὐτὴ ἡ ἀλήθεια. ὥσε πρῶτον μεν ταύτη ἀκ ὀρθῶς εἰσηγῇ, εἰσηγούμενος τῆς των πολλῶν δόξης δειν ἡμᾶς Φροντιζειν περί των δικαίων καί καλῶν καὶ ἀγαθῶν, καί των ἐναντίων.

YARMOUTH:
PRINTED BY DOWNES AND MARCH,
For Meſſrs. ROBINSONS, and T. BECKET, LONDON;
And ELLIOT and KAY, EDINBURGH.

M. DCC. XCI.

THE

PRINCIPLES

OF

GOVERNMENT,

DELINEATED.

PART THE FIRST,

ON

CIVIL GOVERNMENT.

—— *et ordinem*
Rectum evaganti frena licentiæ
Injecit, ——

           —— *non. furor*
Civilis, aut vis exiget OTIUM
Non ira, quæ procudit enses
Et miseras inimicat urbes.

           HOR.

LETTERS

TO THE

Rev. Dr. PRIESTLEY.

LETTER I.

SIR,

AS soon as I had read *Mr. Burke's* justly celebrated "*Reflections*," I entertained no doubt, but that you would attempt to answer them, before I saw your declaration of such an intention, publickly announced in the newspapers. Do not however imagine, that I am so absurd as to think, that such a discovery is a proof either of any uncommon sagacity, or laborious application of mind; as it only required for it's foundation, some attention to

A

the

the ideal channels, through which, your multifarious writings have generally flowed. For even a very flight obfervation, is all which is neceffary to enable any one to difcover, that you are *(in Bifhop Warburton's phrafe)* *" An Anfwerer by Profeffion,"* to every work, written in defence of the prefent civil and ecclefiaftical government of this country. A conftitution of government, which under the liberal fhelter of it's wide extended branches protefts you, from every ftorm and blaft of perfecution; and affords to every unhappy wanderer in exile, or even outcaft from all religions, a fecure retreat, in which, he may eat his bread in comfort, peace, liberty, and fafety.

I have now at length read your promifed publication, though I was for fome time prevented by a variety of avocations, from indulging myfelf in that pleafure, for which I fo eagerly wifhed. And, as I had not been before deceived in my expeftation,

of

of feeing *some* anfwer from you; fo likewife I am not now in the leaft difappoint-
ed, in finding it to be, *fuch* an anfwer, as
it is. For, exactly the fame obfervation,
which fupplied me with the grounds of probability for the one, equally furnifhed me
with the means of conjecturing, what would
be the materials, and texture of the other.

But, impatient however as I was to examine the work itfelf; my attention was
for fome time unwillingly detained, in the
contemplation of the *mottos* which adorn
the title-page. For I have been totally at
a lofs to conceive, what could poffibly be
your intention, purport, or defign, in blazoning the front of your pamphlet with
thofe fentences. The moft proper motive,
which, I conceive, can prompt a writer to
prefix a motto to a work; is, to induce
his readers to embrace the fentiments which
he holds, by fhowing, that they are likewife the opinions of another, to whom, from

a juftly acquired authority, more deference is due, than to the author himfelf. But this motive appears to me, to be totally inapplicable to the prefent cafe. Becaufe, the mottos were taken from Mr. Burke's *own "Reflections,"* which it was your pro-feffed defign to refute; and confequently therefore to prove them to be fo far from having any claim to deference, that they were not even entitled to any one's affent. But, with this defign in view, to quote Mr. Burke as an *Oracle,* from whofe fen-tence there was no appeal; feems to me to be as unaccountable a conduct, as his would be, who, after having boafted of his fkill and courage, and even challenged ano-ther to a duel, fhould, at the very moment, he was accoutred for the combat, inftantly confefs the invincible powers of his anta-gonift, feize his adverfary's fword, and by plunging it into his own breaft, commit a defperate act of fuicide.

What

What then Sir, could poffibly be your intention, in quoting thefe fentences, or axioms from Mr. Burke, appears to me to be totally inexplicable, upon any principles of reafon, and found fenfe. To evince, that this declaration neither contains an affertion deftitute of proof, nor implies a cenfure unfupported by juftice, permit me, to tranfcribe the mottos.

" *Eloquence may exift without a proportion-*
"*able degree of wifdom.*"

" *Steady independent minds, when they have*
" *an object of fo ferious a concern to man-*
" *kind as* GOVERNMENT, *under their con-*
" *templation, will difdain to affume the part*
" *of* SATIRISTS *and* DECLAIMERS."

As to the *latter* motto, it is I muft confefs, the very laft, which I fhould have conceived, *prudence* would have fuffered you to have chofen. For it can ferve no

other

other purpofe, than to fhow, that you ftand
felf condemned by your own quotations;
as every one at all converfant with your
writings, muft know, that they *abound* in
fatire and declamation upon the government
of your country; if indeed it be admitted,
that compofitions are entitled to thofe appellations, which contain grofs invectives
without wit, and bold affertions without
elegance.

As to the FIRST, that, " *eloquence* MAY
exift *without a proportionable degree of wifdom*," this is certainly as true, as that Mr.
Burke poffeffes one of the higheft degrees
of eloquence, which was ever the portion
of any human mind. And confequently, fuch
a maxim coming from one fo well qualified
by his own unrivalled eloquence and confum-
mate wifdom, to form a judgement upon
this point, it muft neceffarily make a very
forcible impreffion upon the minds of others.
But then, the quotation ftill only ferves to
promulgate

promulgate *Mr. Burke's* AUTHORITY, NOT
YOURS; the latter of which in this cafe,
required fupport, even to the demolition of
his. Was the infertion of it then owing, to
one of thofe miftakes, to which you have
been fo fubject, in your " *Corruptions of the*
" *Hiftory of Chriftianity ?*" I beg your pardon, I believe the *title*, which you give to
it, is, the *Hiftory of the Corruptions of Chri-*
" *ftianity.*

    It may be poffible, that in the " *rapid*
" *glance,*" which according to your ufual
practice, you took of Mr. Burke's book,
you read it THUS, " *eloquence* NEVER EX-
" ISTS *with a proportionate degree of wifdom.*"
If this was the fact, *then* indeed you have
quoted it with the moft fingular propriety;
as thinking, you condemned Mr. Burke out
of his own mouth. But then your print-
er, by correcting the miftake in the words
of the fentence, has moft unfortunately obliterated all meaning from it's application.
Or,

Or, did the miftake arife, not from any imperfection in your SIGHT, but from the much greater misfortune, of a cataract form-ing upon your REASON? Did you conclude, that if, eloquence MAY exift without a pro-portionable degree of knowledge, it necef-farily MUST do fo in *Mr. Burke?* Now though this can never be admitted as a legitimate deduction, till every juft princi-ple of *logic* be firft deftroyed, yet even an affent to this inference, would neither di-minifh Mr. Burke's authority, nor increafe yours. For even ftrip him of all his elo-quence, which kills at every ftroke, and leave him only his wifdom; he would ftill be but like Pallas robbed of her fpear, but whofe Ægis alone will ftrike her op-ponents dumb in confufion, horror, and difmay.*   But

* Mr. Burke will I hope excufe me if I make an exception, in refpect to the impeachment of Mr. Haftings, where he feems to have dipped the point of his fpear in venom, and to have thrown away his fhield.

But perhaps, as none of the fuppofitions which I have already made, can furnifh even a fhadow of a reafon for your adoption of this firft motto ; there may ftill be another inference, which you may have deduced from it, which may appear to you, to evince the much greater deference due to the authority of your name, than to that of Mr. Burke. For, as it is allowed, that eloquence MAY EXIST without a *proprotionable* degree of wifdom, you may perhaps therefore conclude, that in that mind, in which, NO ELOQUENCE EXISTS, there MUST BE the HIGHEST DEGREE of WISDOM. And indeed, if this did not happen to be an inference, which a Tyro in the Soph's Schools at Cambridge, would laugh at as a deduction from fuch premifes, (no wonder therefore you lament in your letters, that the youth of your perfuafion are not admitted into our Univerfities) it would undoubtedly, hold forth to you, the palm of fuperiority, and the garland of victory. For

B   though

though it muſt be confeſſed, that numbers can not forbear to lament, that your writings are much too barren in argument, too fertile in invective, and too copious in aſſertion,—it muſt likewiſe be acknowledged, that no one was ever daring enough, to have the injuſtice to accuſe you, of exhibiting in them at any time, even the fainteſt glimmer, of the dimmeſt ray of ELOQUENCE.

What renders this laſt conjecture of mine, the more probable, is, that this deduction which I now ſuppoſe you to have made, appears to be not only a current opinion, but even an univerſally received axiom amongſt all thoſe living authors, who are either honoured with encomiums from your pen, or who offer up incenſe at your ſhrine.

It was indeed formerly ſuppoſed, that an UNION, of the faculties of MEMORY, IMAGINATION, WIT, JUDGEMENT, REASONING,

REASONING, SAGACITY, INTELLECT, and of INVENTION, long employed in deep thinking and profound inveſtigation, could alone qualify any one to become a writer; and that as every man's ſmalleſt pretence to literary reputation, muſt be founded upon ſome participation of theſe qualities, ſo, the reſpective degrees in fame, to which different individuals were entitled, muſt be eſtimated, by the various rays, into which their genius could be reſolved, when diſentangled from the almoſt infinite variety of modes of combination, in which thoſe rays are capable of being blended.

Upon theſe principles it is, that HOMER and VIRGIL, DEMOSTHENES and CICERO, SOCRATES, PLATO, and ARISTOTLE, SHAKESPEAR and MILTON, BACON and BERKLEY, NEWTON and LOCKE, muſt be elevated to the higheſt ſeats in the temple of fame.

B 2   But,

But, the great LIBERALITY of SENTI-
MENT, of the prefent age, of which, we
hear from you, and other writers, fuch
frequent and juſt encomiums, has, very
kindly difpenfed with the neceſſity, of fet-
ting forth a title to genius, by means, which
demand fo much labour from the claim-
ants, and require fo much nice difcrimi-
nation in the judges. For, the prefent enlightened age, juſtly fo denominated as every
fchool boy knows upon claſſical authority,
(as, *Lucus a non lucendo,*) have found, fome
nearer, though crooked and fubterraneous
paths to the temple of fame. By paſſing
along thefe, and by frequent and importu-
nate applications at the doors of fome of
the lower offices of the fane, they gain free
admittance, and are foon led up by a fe-
cret afcent into the moſt fpacious and
fplendid apartments of the place. Whilſt
they, who by the *plain* and *direct* path approach the central door, which always ſtands
open, and enter without courting the por-
ter,

ter, are obliged to remain crouded in the narrow entries and paffages of. the edifice. But no fooner has Death with Time afferted their claims, than the latter, by their ætherial nature mount aloft, and are then venerated as the guides, the guardians, and enlighteners, of mankind. Whilft the putrid carcafes of the former, are thrown out in fcornful filence, to be devoured by the fowls of. the air, and the beafts of the field, unlefs fome future author, fhould from mere. pity and compaffion, afterwards gather their fcattered limbs together;—place them in the niches of fome future *Biographia::Britannica,*—and embalm them,—with all the gums and unguents,—which befmear the bodies of Egyptian Kings.

This is one of the happy improvements, which we owe, to the flood of light, poured in upon us, in modern times. So that even you Sir, who, are now upon thefe principles, upborn upon the ftrongeft waxened

wings

wings of modern fame, and who, if we believe your own writings, are much wifer than the Apoftles; even you, need never to be in fear, left you fhould be rebuked with the cenfure that the apoftle Paul was, that *" much learning has made you mad."*

But, were there indeed another GREY to appear, who had with much application fo ftrengthened, and cultivated his native vigour, as with eafe to vault upon the back of Pegafus, and could turn and manage him as he pleafed; HE would be hooted at by the majority, and miftaken for a Centaur. Or, were another BERKELEY to arife, and pour forth the ftreams which he had imbibed from the very depth of the Pierian Spring, too refined for the tafte, and too fubtle for the palate of modern times; his genius, would with all the delicacy of modern wit be ridiculed; and his infpirations be ftigmatized, and condemned, as the intoxicating fumes of the

infpiring

infpiring Bacchus, or as the frantic ravings
of the Pythian Prieftefs.

Though the difcovery, which I have already related, be certainly the brighteft
which has been made by the moderns, yet
it muft not be concealed, that there is
another, which indeed followed from it as
a confequence; and which truly if not
quite fo ingenious, is at leaft equally ufeful.

For it has been found, that the world is
at prefent fo faturated with knowledge and
wifdom, that BOOK-WRITING is no longer
therefore of any value; and it has therefore been ingenioufly refolved to fubftitute,
in it's place,—BOOK-MAKING. Nothing certainly can redound more to the honour of
the *humanity* of the prefent times, than
this refolution of faving all expence of
thought, and confequently all the fatigue
of mind, and maceration of the body; which

fo

fo much harraffed the antients. For by this admirable difcovery, every one now who can but read, is rendered qualified at once, to become a critic, and an author.

In the fcience of BOOK-MAKING, there are however certainly two degrees, which are often confounded by the vulgar. For, the fame terms of commendation, viz. of ingenuity, and of learning, are often indifcriminately beftowed upon both; not a doubt being entertained whether thofe terms, are with juftice, applicable to either. The one fpecies, fo little requires the ufe of a pen; that any one who was never even taught to write, may rife in it, to the very apex of fame. A ftrong inftrument of iron, whether fafhioned into the form of a knife, or of fciffars, if it be but able to cut the works of other writers in pieces, and fome flour and water, condenfed into pafte firm enough to join together again the " *disjecti* " *Membra Poetæ,*" are all the acquifitions
which

which are requifite for any one, who would
reach the higheft excellence in this branch
of the art. The other, it muft be confeffed, demands from it's cultivators, a little
more labour. For in this cafe, the perfon
who would impart food to others, muft
firft fwallow it himfelf; and then, before
it has at all contributed to his own nu-
trition, he muft with fome pains and ftrug-
gles difgorge it, and arrange it in fome
decent order, fo that the heterogeneous
morfels may not offend the ftomachs of
his guefts. Or, perhaps, this latter fpecies
of BOOK-MAKING, may with more decorum
be compared, to thofe pafteboards which
are invented for the ufe of children, and
are called *geographical diffected maps*. Thefe,
whilft they are fhut up in their boxes, are
a mere " *rudis indigeftaque Moles*," exactly
refembling the juxta pofition of the ideas
of a book-maker, while depofited in his memory; but both which, the moft ignorant,
may by a very flight operation, and con-

C   fequently

fequently one very eafily learned, without knowing any thing of the boundaries and relations of countries in the one, or of the connection between the fciences in the other, arrange in fuch order, as to teach fome-thing at leaft by this mechanic procefs; which, the weaknefs of the learners intel-lects, would be incapable of acquiring, by a fcientific progreffion.

I truft Sir, that YOU, do not conceive me to be at all wandering from the parti-cular fubject of my addrefs, by this fhort, but juft account of the difcoveries of mo-dern authors; as it has certainly the clof-eft connection with your Letters to *Mr. Burke.** He being a writer entitled to fame,
only

* By modern Authors, I hope it will be un-derftood, I mean only, certain writers in the South-ern parts of this Ifle. For, in the more Northern, the Authors when they err, err ingenioufly; ftill continuing to habituate themfelves to much deep
thinking;

only upon the old exploded claim of the antients. Whilft you, Sir, are at once the great difcoverer, and grand exemplar of the much more illuftrious modification of the claim, by the moderns. You ftanding indifputably the firft in fame amongft the prefent clafs of writers, which I have been laft defcribing; not only for the excellence, but likewife, without even excepting Dr. Hill of famous memory, for the multiplicity, and multifarioufnefs of your works.

But fhould you perchance at prefent, deny that there is any connection, between this delineation and the fubject of your letters, I do not defpair in my progrefs, to make even *you* for once confefs, that *you* are *miftaken;* notwithftanding your conftant habit of congratulating yourfelf upon a vic-

C 2   tory,

thinking; they have as yet exhibited, but few traits of their neighbours wonderful improvements, in the craft, art, trade, and myftery of BOOK-MAKING.

tory, and of ordering your followers to fing *Io Pæan*, when all the reft of the world are witneffes of your defeat.* I am perfuaded the film will foon be fo entirely removed from before your eyes, that you will fee, " *Luce clarius*," that the foregoing obfervations, not only form a proper introduction to an examination of your letters, but that the examination itfelf, will likewife illuftrate, and confirm the obfervations. Both of them, by their mutual attraction, giving durability to each others cohefion, and adding folidity to each others weight.

Before, however, I conclude this letter, it may not perhaps be unneceffary to obviate a charge, with which, I may very probably be arraigned in my account of the

* See the Controverfy between the Bifhop of St. David, and Dr. Prieftley.

the genius, and invention, of the prefent times. To have paffed by unnoticed, the purfuits of ELECTRICITY and CHEMISTRY, which not only fo much occupy the attention of the prefent age, but which, it is conceived, will entitle it to the higheft celebrity in future times, it will perhaps be faid, could only arife either from the groffeft igno-rance, or the moft flagrant injuftice. But I can moft folemnly affure fuch accufers, that no one, is more ready than I am, to beftow on fuch refearches, all the praife which is due to them; and that no one would more rejoice than I fhould, to fee them fo far purfued, that from the col-lection of a multitude of particular facts, fuch principles fhall be educed, as will fupply firm foundations, for the erection of thofe fafhionable ftudies, into *fabrics* of *fci-ence*. Though I cannot however forbear at the fame time, moft fincerely to lament, that other fciences have hitherto received much injury from the prefent fond predilection,

lection, and warm partiality in favour of
thofe purfuits. For, whilft their almoft bigotted admirers, have had, not the work of
Architects, but only as it were of *Labour-
ers* to perform, having had more call for
the ufe of their hands and eyes, than of
their REASON and INTELLECT, yet the
fame which has been beftowed upon them
by the kind indulgence of a partial public,
has fo inflated them with the conceit of
their own merit, greatnefs, and importance,
as to make them think themfelves entitled
to dogmatize upon far different fubjects,
which are founded upon a very different
fpecies of knowledge, than what they have
really acquired; and requires the employment of very different faculties, from thofe,
which they were wont to exercife. This
falfe conceit however, it muft be confeffed,
ought not to be confidered as the peculiar
characteriftic of this age and country. For
though now BERKELEY is gone, we fhall
fearch in vain for *another Plato*, yet even
in

in this divine Philofopher's time, we find, that the fame partiality for experiments upon fenfible objeɛts, had occafioned the fame delirium at Athens, as it has fince produced in England. For, HE tells us, there were even then, SOME MEN, who FANCIED themfelves to be PHILOSOPHERS, " *who would not believe,* THAT *could be* ANY-" THING, *which they could not* GRASP *with* " *their* HANDS, *and who would not liften to* " *a Philofopher, who fpoke to them of* ANY-" THING, *which was* NOT BODY." *

I am, Sir,

Yours, &c.

---

* See Plato in Sophifta, and Prieftley's Difquifition on Matters and Spirit, &c.

ERRATUM.—Page 10, laft l. after *Imagination,* add TASTE.

LETTER

LETTER II.

SIR,

THOUGH I am fo unfortunate, as to entertain an opinion, that your firft, and fecond Letter, refemble batteries, which are fo feeble in their conftruction, and fo ill fupplied with ammunition, that an adverfary may fafely pafs them by, regardlefs of every annoyance, they can poffibly give to his forces in their march,—I truft to your *good nature*, and *meeknefs* for pardon. For, if I fhould boldly advance with my troops, at once to attack your principal forts, there to encounter your utmoft ftrength, and fhould mifcarry in my defign; mine, would be, the defeat, and fhame; yours, the

triumph,

triumph, and glory. Should I however fucceed, I fhall perhaps return, and then demolifh thofe batteries; which, for their weaknefs, I before neglected; and if I am right in my firft conjecture, I fhall, I think, find, that mere firing off fome of their guns, will caufe them to tumble into pieces, even by the mere force of the recoil.

ONE of your PRINCIPAL FORTS, which by ftanding firft, is moft prominent to the fight, is called, " THE NATURE OF GOVERN- " MENT, OR THE RIGHTS OF MEN AND OF " KINGS." Now the forces, which you have brought together, as the fole fupport, upon which you rely for it's defence; feem to be, the moft extraordinary, that *any* one who vaunts himfelf upon his abilities, as a ge- neral, could poffibly have felected. And even ftill more extraordinary is it, that of all men, YOU, in particular, fhould have chofen them, who pride yourfelf upon al-

D   ways

ways carrying on *your polemics*, under the ban-
ner of REASON. For, it is, by that *power's*
peculiar predilection for you, the supplies
which it lends to you alone, and it's pa-
noply with which it has always covered you,
that you boast, you have become victorious
in all your engagements, and have tram-
pled underfoot,—Infidels,—Jews,—Christians,
—Bishops,—and Apostles.

But, it is now time perhaps, to drop
all metaphor; and quote the plain language (for so it is in this place) of your
Pamphlet.

You begin, with telling Mr. Burke, that,
" considering how much has been written
" on the subject of government, since the
" revolution in this country, which more
" than any thing contributed to open the
" eyes of Englishmen, with respect to the
" true principles of it, it is not a little
" extraordinary that any man of *reading*
" and

" and *reflection* as he is, fhould depart
" from them fo much as he has done."

' The only obfervation, which I fhall make
upon this paffage at prefent, is, that the
inferting of the word " *Reflection*" which it
contains; feems to have arifen from a mere
flip of your pen. For, we muft neceffarily infer, only from the next paragraph
but one; that you do NOT think it *extraordinary*, that Mr. Burke, fhould have
deviated from thofe principles, by the aid
of " *Reflection*;" but, that as this was in
reality, the caufe of his departure from
them: that he is in your opinion, for
that very reafon, deferving of cenfure,—
becaufe he *did reflect* upon them, and not
take them *for granted;* as *you* think, he
ought to have done.

For, after laying down what you fuppofe
to be the fundamental principle of government, according to Lord Somers, Mr. Locke,

and

and Bifhop Hoadley, you fay, (addreffing
yourfelf to Mr. Burke.)

. " You, Sir, do not directly, and in fo
" many words deny thefe great principles
" of all government, or the general con-
" clufion drawn from them. In fact, you
" admit them *all* when you allow, page 87,
" that *civil fociety* is made for the *advantage*
" of man." " But you advance what is re-
" ally inconfiftent with thefe leading prin-
" ciples, and you would *tie up our hands*
" from making any *effectually ufe of them.*
" You feem to have forgotten, what you
" muft have formerly learned; but *it is*
" *too late for us to go to fchool* again, and
" *relearn the firft elements of political fcience.*
" What our *predeceffors* took great pains to
" PROVE, *we now* receive as AXIOMS, and
" WITHOUT HESITATION ACT *upon them.*"

Now, however divided men may be in
their fentiments upon this Paragraph, in,
refpect

respect to it's truth, so far as it contains
a charge against Mr. Burke, and the reasons upon which, you have grounded it;
yet I doubt not, but they will be as una-
nimously, free from hesitation, in *believing*
this last declaration, of yours, respecting
yourself and your friends, as you, and any
of them can possibly be in *making* and
acting, in the strictest conformity with it.

In reference to Mr. Burke, this Paragraph certainly, upon first " *looking through*
" *it,*" appears to accuse him only of *for-
getfulness* of those principles, which you
suppose him to have forsaken. But if, to
our looking, we add the slightest consideration upon it, we see most clearly, that
it also contains (as I just now hinted) an
equal condemnation of him, if upon RE-
FLECTION HE has *changed* those sentiments,
which YOU STILL *maintain.* For, by the
declaration of your own conduct, you censure that man as unwise, who examines afterwards

terwards, what he was taught at school, and condemn it as an impropriety in an old man, even to DOUBT the truth of an opinion, which, he had learned, when he was a boy. This certainly is an idea, diametrically oppofite to the fentiments, and practice of the wifeft of the antients, which likewife every fchool-boy muft have been taught, who, has made even but a very fmall progrefs in learning; but, which it feems, YOU, YOURSELF with all your predilection for your infant knowledge, and cenfure, upon Mr. Burke, for his fuppofed failing in this refpect;—have either forgotten, or difcarded.

Whether therefore, Mr. B's dereliction of his youthful principles, have arifen from the fterility of his prefent memory, or the copioufnefs of his manly Reflections, neither caufe, is fufficiently unufual, to excite either wonder, or furprife. The one, I muft confefs, from the vaft treafures, which

we

we fee Mr. B. continually bringing forth
from the repofitory of his memory, does
not appear to me, to be the real caufe,
though you have affigned it. And the
other, has always been efteemed, deferving of the higheft approbation, except by
Popes and *Cardinals*, 'till *you* condemned
it. That *they* fhould feel a diflike to fuch
a conduct, we cannot wonder, becaufe there
feems to be the moft perfect *elective at-*
traction, between that fentiment, and their
other religious opinions. But that you, Sir,
fhould exprefs the flighteft tendency to fuch
a fentiment, that you fhould embrace fuch
a tenet, and deliver fuch a dogma, as the
quotation from your own letter contains,
muft excite in every one, not only the
higheft degree of furprife, but likewife of
aftonifhment. You, Sir, whofe other principles and conduct are of fuch a kind, that
not only fuch a fentiment, can never produce with them, the fmalleft effect of a
chemical folution, but muft by their mutual

tual repulfion burft the containing veffel.
You, Sir, whofe *theological* lucubrations are
founded upon a · maxim, the · very *reverfe*
of this; I mean, the · *actually unlearning*, as
you advance into the winter of age, ALL that
you were taught, in the feafon of youth.

It would be a curious fpeculation to
inveftigate, and I doubt not but noble
fruit, would be the reward of the labour,
were any one to difcover, from whence
has arifen this inveterate prejudice of yours,
in favour of the writers upon *government*,
and your prejudice equally ftrong againft
the writers, upon the *New Teftament ?*
What has made you, a thus open and
declared *bigot* to the *infallibility* of LOCKE,
and ftill more and more a *fceptic* as to
the *authority* of CHRIST, and his APOS-
TLES? Surely we may apply to you the
obfervation of Horace, " nil fuit unquam
" tam impar fibi;" for, without meaning to
give you any offence, fuch a character muft
be

be uncommon; and whatever is uncommon, usually excites our admiration.

But Sir, I can so easily conceive, that Mr. Burke may differ from *Mr. Locke's* principles in his treatise on government, without *forgetting* them, that I am utterly unable to conceive, how they can possibly be admitted by any one, who has been previously habituated to much thought and deep reflection, before he happens to read them, either in consequence of his own choice, or in obedience to the command of his tutor. That Mr. Locke, must always stand deservedly very high, in the temple of fame, it would be folly or injustice to deny. But, that he was *not* ALWAYS *clear* in his *first principles,* nor *right* in his *deductions* from them, even in ANY of his works, and *more particularly* in those, upon CIVIL GOVERNMENT, may be asserted with truth, because it is capable of demonstration. And I must confess, I was

E   scarcely

ſcarcely ever more ſurpriſed in my life, when upon reading the ingenious " Eſſays, " (entitled) *philoſophical, hiſtorical,* and *moral,*" I found the Author, I do not mean combating the lively remarks of *Soam Jenyns,* for they are more ludicrous, than convincing; but ſeriouſly defending Locke's notions; " THAT ALL MEN ARE BORN FREE," and alſo " EQUAL;" who at the ſame time, with ſo much ingenuity of obſervation, and force of argument, has refuted what *he* terms, " *the groſs error,*" and the " *egregious blunders*" of Dr. Price.

This ſuppoſed *natural freedom,* and *natural equality* of mankind, are the ſources from which thoſe NATURAL RIGHTS muſt be drawn, of which we hear ſo much, but have been taught ſo little; and which, when the modern great advocates for them, are urged to explain,—inſtead of defining,—they content themſelves with only repeating the words

words over again,—without giving us the flighteft elucidation of their meaning.

Now Sir, as you have not ventured yourfelf down the well, where, truth is faid to keep her refidence at the bottom, and drawn up from thence, *firft* principles for yourfelf; permit me for a time, to take my leave of you, and to accompany Mr. Locke, for whofe abilites, I have the higheft refpeft, though I am not, as you are, "*addiƈtus jurare in verba Magiftri.*"

I am, Sir,

Yours, &c.

P. S. You will, I hope, excufe the liberty I have taken, in tranfpofing the order, in which, the names of Locke and Hoadley, ftand in your letter. For, though I have a great refpeft for high rank, I have,

E 2

a much greater veneration for fuperior genius; and therefore I did not choofe, to put
as you have done, the fcholar before the
mafter. Locke was certainly, a great genius,
and though I am not difpofed, in imitation
of you and the Perfians, to worfhip the
fun;—yet, I confider the rays of Locke's
genius, as collected into a focus in his
writings, imparting light to Bifhop Hoadley,
—like, the beams of the heavenly luminary,
concentred in a convex glafs,—kindling into
a *contention*,—between blaze and fmoke,—
fome of the *mere common ftubble* of the *field.*

LETTER

L E T T E R   III.

SIR,

I Muſt beg leave to obſerve, that from the firſt moment of my taſting Mr. Locke's principles upon government, they never appeared to me, to have by any means the ſame flavour, with thoſe which come from the well of truth. For when, having firſt carefully ſeparated the ideas annexed, to the words,—" the *natural freedom* and *equa-* " *lity* of *mankind*," from all the extraneous matter mixed with them, and we have put them into a well-cloſed alembic,—we ſhall find the *precipitation* to conſiſt, only of this ſimple, inſipid, *identical propoſition*, as the Logicians term it. Viz. that *whilſt* men

live

live in a *state* of *nature*,—which is *prior* to
the exiſtence of what we call *civil government*, mens actions are not under any of
thoſe POLITICAL reſtraints, nor have men
themſelves THOSE *diſtinctions* of ſtation, which
are *created*, when a government is eſtabliſhed;—which is in fact, only to ſay,—that
a ſtate of nature, and a ſtate of government, are *not one*, and the *ſame* ſtate, but
different ones :—And that the former is
therefore, without all rules, laws, and re-
gulations, which exiſt in the latter. Certainly no ghoſt was wanted to tell us this,
becauſe it is implied in the very DEFI-
NITIONS of the TERMS. But, I cannot
conceive in what *other* ſenſe than the foregoing, it can be ſaid, that " *men are born free*,"
except it be in this,—which is as little to the
purpoſe,—that NATURE, or more properly
the GOD of NATURE, has endowed them with
FREE-WILL, or a POWER of chooſing one
thing, in preference to another. This indeed,

is

is certainly very true, and is therefore admitted; but the sole question, relative to the NATURAL FREEDOM of mankind, is, his *natural* freedom, as to the REAL EXERCISE of the POWER of ACTING, in CONSEQUENCE of SUCH a CHOICE. And this, it is manifest, is much less in a *man's* power *in* a *state* of *nature*, than even in a *state* of *society*. And consequently his NATURAL, is for the most part less, than his POLITICAL freedom. For this is the very circumstance, which from the first exercise of reason, upon long continued experience, prompts men to unite together, and willingly to submit to any, even the *most burdensome restraints*, which the very *worst species* of *civil government*, can possibly lay upon them, as far preferable, to those evils, which they endured in that state of *anarchy*, called, a *state of nature*.

For, it may, with a much nearer approach to truth, be said, of almost any

other

other animal, that he is born to *act* as he chufes; than of MAN. Man being of all animals, *that, which* is, from the *neceffities* of his nature in the greateft degree, and for the longeft time, not merely *accidentally,* but even *neceffarily fubject* to the *authority,—will,* —and *controul* of it's parents; and which fubjection continues in a ftate of nature even ftill longer, than in a ftate of fociety. But when he even becomes emancipated, from that fubjection, is he not ftill liable to be thwarted in the indulgence of his wifhes, and the execution of his intentions, by every one, and therefore fubject to the controul of every one, who is either *ftronger,* more *fkilful,* or more *cunning* than himfelf? For will any one contend, that all men are *born,* and *continue* equal in thefe qualities; any more than in thofe of ftature, ftraitnefs and beauty? In *what refpect* then, can we find men *born* EQUAL? And confequently in what *other* fenfe, than in the quibbling kind of fenfe. (You will be

fo

fo good as to remember the quibble is not mine, but Mr. Locke's,) which I have before mentioned, can they be faid to be *born* FREE ?

Befides, it is not only from each féparate individual, who is ftronger than himfelf, that a man's aftions are liable to controul, in a *ftate* of *nature;* but likewife, from every defigned, or cafual *union* of thofe, who may *each* of them, bo *individually* WEAKER.

For pleafe to look into the country, and there fee horfes,—cows,—fheep,—and oxen,—turned into their different paftures;—even amongft them, you will find fome *one,* of each fpecies, at firft trying his ftrength, and afterwards becoming lord, and mafter over the reft. If one alone however, fhould prove to be unequal to the conqueft, you will behold then, *fome* of the ftronger,—by union with each other,—keep-

F   ing

ing the weaker at a diſtance,—and forcing
them to be content,—with the very worſt
paſture in the field, whilſt the tyrants feed
where they pleaſe, and monopolize to themſelves, the beſt and ſweeteſt of the graſs.
Take a view of them ſome time afterwards,—when they have gorged themſelves
to the full, in the favourite ſpot,—and
ſpoiled what they have not eaten,—you
will then ſee them driving away the others
from the place, where they had before
permitted them to graze,—and for a time,
will take poſſeſſion of it for themſelves.
Juſt ſo, turn out *men* alſo, upon the great
COMMON of nature, i. e. conceive them
to be placed in a *ſtate* of *nature*, and in
what, will conſiſt the difference of their
conduct, from that of other animals? In
nothing but this,—that in proportion,—as
they have a greater ability, to contrive
various means of gratifying their paſſions,
—proud, covetous, and domineering over
their ſpecies, as other animals may be;

MEN

MEN WILL BE,—ſtill MORE haughty,—
MORE avaricious,—and MORE tyrannical.

Totally unacquainted therefore, with the
FIRST PRINCIPLES of GOVERNMENT, do
all thoſe appear to me to be, who ſuppoſe it to be founded upon the HAPPI-
NESS, ariſing from this NATURAL *freedom,*
and NATURAL *equality* of mankind, if any
can be guilty of ſuch an abuſe of words,
as ſo to call them. Conſequently therefore
moſt egregiouſly miſtaken muſt they be,
who in the moſt crab-like, and retrograde
procedure, are continually meaſuring back,
the RELATIVE PERFECTION of each government; by the degrees of it's approxi-
mation, to man's imagined ORIGINAL
FREEDOM, and EQUALITY in a *ſtate of
nature.*

Where then are we to find, that root
of NATURAL RIGHTS, from which, we
have been told, the trunk and branches
of

of all good governments, muſt originally derive, their ſturdy vigour, and umbrageous ſhade.

Perhaps it will be urged, in defence of Mr. Locke; for *you* are not *ſingular* in preferring the *authority* of a *name*, to the *force* of an *argument;*—that though it may be granted,—that ſuch is the turbulence, and violence of a *ſtate of nature*, that in it, man cannot be ſaid to be *born* indeed, to the *actual exerciſe* of freedom; yet nevertheleſs, he may be truly ſaid, to be born with a RIGHT to freedom of action, in conſequence of his free-will.

But, this, is only the ſame as to ſay, in other words, that all men have a RIGHT upon all occaſions, when . they chooſe it, to do wrong,—though, all men when they chooſe it, have a RIGHT to prevent it. For, if every man has a right to every thing he CHOOSES, then it follows, that

every

every man has a *right* to hurt, or kill every man, when he chooſes; though every man chooſing *not* to be hurt, or killed, has an equal *right* to reſiſt. If this be not NON-SENSE, I muſt confeſs, I know not, WHAT IS. So that at laſt, all this cloud of duſt, which has been raiſed by the puffing advocates, for the NATURAL RIGHTS OF MEN, ſettles into this *identical* propoſition, only that man in a ſtate of nature, *can do* a thing, when he has a *power to do it:* or that when he is *not controuled,* he is *free* to *act.*

For, ſuppoſe a man in a ſtate of nature, ſhould attempt to perform an action, which, a ſtronger man than he, FORBIDS him to do, upon pain of loſing his life; —what LAW,—what AUTHORITY,—what RULE,—what PRESCRIPTION,—what PER-MISSION, can the weaker plead, for doing it? If, for inſtance, as he is about to carry home the animal, which he himſelf

had

had killed in the chace, another who is
ftronger, and has been hunting with him,
chufes to take it from him, what PLEA of
RIGHT can the former ufe? If he fhould
urge, that he is hungry, the latter may
ufe exactly the fame plea. If the one plead
his labour, and danger in going out in
purfuit of it; the other may plead, his
equal labour and danger in both thefe
circumftances. If the one, plead his RIGHT
to it, from KILLING it; the other may
with juft as much reafon, claim it on the
plea, of his VICTORY, in TAKING it from
him. For, if, he who killed it, urge as a
plea, that it is his PROPERTY, becaufe he
killed it; then, this affertion is either abfurd, or muft imply fome CONVENTION;
and confequently, fome SPECIES of GO-
VERNMENT amongft certain perfons; who,
have *agreed* to fuffer every one to enjoy
unmolefted, the prey, which *he* himfelf has
killed. For without fuch a *convention*, NO
PROPERTY can poffibly exift; and confequently

quently therefore NO RIGHT, previous to fome league or covenant between men, which fome have agreed to adhere to, and to fupport, by fome *common* FORCE, againft *any* infringement;—which union conftitutes a fpecies of *government*. From nature then, men may have POSSESSIONS; but it is from GOVERNMENT alone, they can derive their CLAIM to them,—as RIGHTS.

I too well know already, and I fear I fhall experience it yet more fully, how extremely difficult, it is fo far to *over-come* men's PREPOSSESSIONS, much more, to conquer their PREJUDICES, fo as to make them, *accurately*, and *clearly* to dif-cern, the GROUNDS and PRINCIPLES of this reafoning; becaufe, from infancy they learn, to conceive the *practices*, and *prin-ciples*, which are moft *common* in a ftate of government, and fociety, to have univer-fally exifted, *previous* to that ftate. Few, very few, being difpofed to give themfelves

felves the trouble of labouring up to the
fources of *that* NILE, from which, fuch
rules and practifes fpring. Though even, a
poet, I mean, Horace, in his *third fatire*,
might with the aid of a little of their own
reflection, have taught them better. The
paffage begins, " quum prorepferunt primis
" animalia terris." The whole is too long
to tranfcribe, and I fhall therefore refer
you for the remainder, either to the book,
or to your own memory.

From thefe premifes, then, it neceffarily follows; that *before*, we can with any
PROPRIETY, TALK of RIGHTS, we muft
firft fuppofe, fome CLEAR and DEFINITE
RULE of action; by fome means, or other,
to EXIST. For, we can no more fay,
that *any* act is RIGHT, or WRONG, without the exiftence of a RULE of CONDUCT,
with which we can COMPARE it; than we
can fay, a thing is STRAIT or CROOKED,
without MEASURING it, by fome LINE,
either

either fenfible, or imaginary. But in a
MERE STATE of NATURE, who has authority to lay down a rule; by an adherence
to which, or aberration from it, MEN'S
ACTIONS are to be denominated, either
RIGHT, or WRONG? The mere fuppofition
of the exiftence of fuch an authority; is
totally irreconcileable with, contradictory,
and oppofite to the very ideas, which are
comprehended, under the words,—" A STATE
" OF NATURE."

For, where, fuch an *authority* is; there
likewife *fome government* is; and, if, this
authority be in a fingle man, whether it
be vefted in him by others, or ufurped
by himfelf, HE is a MONARCH. If it be
maintained, that though there may be no AU-
THORITY, to command obedience to them,
yet, SUCH RULES may be eftablifhed by
MUTUAL AGREEMENT. We may anfwer,
what does it avail, to lay down a rule,
or rules of conduct, which, no man, is

G   COMPELLABLE

COMPELLABLE to OBEY; becaufe, no man has power to enforce them. For, if you go on further, and fuppofe; that they may, by a mutual compact, *determine* to PUNISH any, who tranfgrefs the rules, to which they have agreed; you once more return to a fuppofition, abfolutely repugnant, to the very idea of a *ftate of nature;* as this, likewife fuppofes a *government.* to *exift;* the fpecies of which, is wholly popular, or in fome meafure, partaking of the republican, oligarchical, or ariftocratical forms.

What therefore, in a STATE OF NATURE, can poffibly give the impulfe to men's actions, (the *lawful authority* of the parent, and *accidental compulfion* of another excepted) but the FIRST PRINCIPLES of our nature; our *inftincts, appetites, defires, paffions;* and the *conclufions* of our *reafon,* as to the *choice,* of the refpective indulgence of them, in any particular cafe? For the

fake

fake of the RECTITUDE, of what RULE,
then, can men by any MOTIVE be induced, to FOREGO, their own indulgence in
any defire they can gratify; though they
fhould even take from another, an objeft
of gratification; which had been ever fo
long in his poffeffion?

If fuch, be the *natural*, and *equal* freedom of all mankind; it is abfurd, to talk
of *rights*, in fuch a ftate; becaufe, it is
only a ftate of *licence*, to every man, to
do hurt to every man, where, his *power*
can fecond his *inclination*.

But, you Sir, and fome others, will perhaps readily fay, that the queftion I have
afked, in the foregoing paragraph, is furely
very eafily refolved: even, without the
neceffity of fuppofing the exiftence of ANY
RULE, to direft men, but merely; by that
very FACULTY of REASON; which I do
not deny, but even have admitted to exift,
in fuch a ftate.

I

I am forry however, to fay, that fuch
an anfwer, would betray a total ignorance,
of the *meaning* of the PRINCIPAL TERM,
which it contains. For, one would think,
as it is here employed, and as indeed, we
hear, and fee numbers, every day, apply-
ing it; that REASON was a *weapon* beftowed upon us, by which, we can, at
any time fubdue the inftinets, defires, inclinations, and paffions of our nature; like
a club, in the hand of a favage; by
which, he may knock down, the beafts of
the foreft. Whereas in truth, the POWER
of REASON, as it relates to our conduct,
is nothing elfe, but that FACULTY, with
which, nature has endowed us, to COM-
PARE the feveral modes of pleafure, and
pain, with each other, which inftigate us
to action; and, fo to enable us, to difcern,
from memory of our paft experience, which
mode in every inftance, furpaffes the reft;
or how each of which, exceeds the other,
in DURATION, and INTENSITY, COMBI-
NED.

NED. When, we make this *comparison*, then, we are said to *reason;* and, if we choose, the acquisition of that pleasure, or the avoidance of that pain, which upon such an estimate, is, the *greatest;* we are said to have made a *rational* choice; or, to *act rationally.* But, whilst men then, have only their instincts, appetites, and passions, to urge them on to action; when no *moral science* exists; when no *law,* nor *rule of action* is instituted, for the direction of man's conduct;—REASON is of *no use* to man, but, to enable him, to *choose* out of those *instincts, appetites,* and *passions, that,* to which in any particular case, he should give the preference to follow; REASON being furnished (in the case supposed) only with the objects of those instincts, &c. out of which, it can direct the will to choose.

Thus for instance, a man may indeed, be sometimes restrained, from forcibly seiz-

ing

ing fomething in the poffeffion of another,
by *dread* of the fuperior ftrength of the individual, at the moment of an open attack;
or deterred, from privately taking it away,
by *fear* of a fpeedy or a lingering RE-
VENGE. For, a STATE OF NATURE, is
only a CONTINUED fcene of CONTENTION,
from OPPOSING PASSIONS.

. But then, though he may certainly here,
very properly be faid to *reafon;* yet, what
conflitutes his *reafoning,* but, the making a
comparifon between the defired good, and
the apprehended .evil? And, what refults
from his reafoning in this cafe, or is the
conclufion of reafon, in refpect to his conduct in this particular inftance? Nothing
but this—that the action is better avoided,
—becaufe, the probability of his incurring
pain by fuch an action, is greater, than
the probability of the acquifition of pleafure: or, that the *rifk* of fuffering the
one, is a greater evil, than the *chance* of
enjoying the other, is a good.

Will

Will you then, Sir, who are not only the difciple of Mr. Locke upon government, but have profeffed to receive HIS OPINIONS as AXIOMS, maintain the EXISTENCE of certain "INNATE MORAL PRACTICAL PRINCIPLES?" You may perhaps, advance fo far, in defence of that fuppofition, and certainly with as much *confiftency* as Mr. Locke has gone, as to fay,—*becaufe*, HE has faid it;—" that NO " MAN, has a RIGHT over the LIFE or " LIBERTY of another, or to hurt him in " *any* refpect whatfoever, unlefs, that *other*, " has *done* SOME HURT to him."

Thefe words, to be fure in themfelves, are no *bad founding words;* but WHAT is their MEANING? Unlefs you can fhow, that the *man himfelf,* has a RIGHT to his LIFE and LIBERTY in a ftate, where, NO LAWS for GOVERNING our PASSIONS exift? For otherwife, they contain only this *identical* propofition; that the *one* man has certainly

certainly NO RIGHT to take them away, becaufe,—NO RIGHT of ANY KIND WHAT-SOEVER, EXISTS. But it is as certain, therefore, that the other upon this ground, can PLEAD NO RIGHT to KEEP them, and confequently, that though the other, inflicts pain, he does NO WRONG IN TAKING THEM AWAY.

But, even, to make out the PROOF of this RIGHT, on the one part, and the WRONG on the other, you perhaps may think to be a moft eafy tafk. For, fo early, was fuch a notion, inftilled into us at firft, and fo continually has it been inculcated into us ever fince, that I doubt not, but many, who do not deem it to be an innate notion, think it to be a felf-evident propofition. You will probably there-fore, think it fufficient to fay, that a man's LIFE and LIBERTY are HIS RIGHTS,—becaufe they are HIS;—they are HIS OWN;—they are HIS PROPERTY;—he is in POS-

SESSION

SESSION of them;—they can not be TA-
KEN from him WITHOUT FORCE;—becaufe,
NATURE has GIVEN them to him, and a
thoufand fuch expreffions, with which we
find the advocates for the *natural rights* of
men adorned; ftrung together like the bead-
ed ornaments of favages, which, like them
too, have only an accidental junction, but
no natural coherence.

For, Sir, the queftion ftill returns, where,
is the *intermediate propofition,* or definition,
which makes RIGHT and POSSESSION in
this cafe, fynonimous terms. NATURE has
given trees; and ftones, poffeffion, of fome
part of the ground; but is a man guilty
of any violation of the RIGHTS of thofe
objects, when he *cuts down a tree, or, forces a ftone to afcend, contrary to it's nature,
into the air.*

But thefe, perhaps you will fay, are
cafes totally diffimilar, becaufe there is NO

H

PAIN produced, in depriving the latter, of
what nature gave them; as there is in the
former case fuppofed. True Sir. Why fuppofe then, that a man in a ftate of nature,
fees an horfe, or a deer, or both, run-
ning wild; and by fome ftratagem he catch-
es them: he certainly immediately deprives
them both of their liberty. Suppofe then
further, that he keeps the one as his flave,
—to lighten his own labour, or,—to give
him pleafure; and that he kills the other for
food,—to gratify his appetite of hunger. Will
you be fo good, as to tell me, whether he
does wrong? If, you, and I can be once convinced, that he does,—I am fure, that neither
of us, fhall, ever again tafte any meat, nor
ever more mount on horfeback, whatever
mortification, from the abftinence, we might
fuftain. Now, Sir, in this cafe, there *is*
PAIN produced, as well as in the cafe before fuppofed; and the horfe's, and deer's
lives, and *liberties*,—were as much *theirs*,—
as much *their own*,—as much *their proper-*

ty

ty,—they were as much in *poſſeſſion* of them,—they had them as much from *nature*, as the man had his. If then, for *theſe* reaſons,—life and liberty were the MAN'S NATURAL RIGHTS,—why are they not equally the NATURAL RIGHTS of the horſe and the deer,—the wolf and the lamb, the fox and the chicken, the dog and the cat; and why is it therefore not as WRONG, to kill even a MOUSE,—as a MAN? Be ſo good, as to *forget* for a moment, that you ever read the BOOK of GENESIS, and then ſhow me, by what *ſingle* principle, or *concatenation* of propoſitions, it follows, that a MAN has a RIGHT to every thing, which nature gave,—of which the deprivation, would give him pain.— I muſt once more tell you,—that I mean, PRIOR to *every inſtitution* of *laws*, and *government*.

For a man to ſay, that as I ſhould feel pain myſelf in ſuch a caſe, therefore,

I will not inflict the pain upon another, but will rather suffer the pain, or inconvenience, I shall myself sustain, from not gratifying my desire, to take away his life and liberty;—would be very excellently humane, and benevolent reasoning, and would apply to all beings, endowed with *sensation*. But this proves not the RIGHT of the ANIMAL, or of the ONE MAN, but only the FORBEARANCE of the OTHER.

Again, suppose he should say, that I am so constituted by nature, that I can not give pain to another sensitive being, without the rebound of some pain upon myself; —therefore I will not be the cause of pain to others? This would certainly evince in him, great sympathy and compassion. But his conduct then would not be founded, upon any sense of the RIGHTS of OTHERS, but upon SELF-LOVE, arising from the consideration of his own susceptibility to pain, under such particular circumstances.

ces. But suppose, his desire of some gratification, which he would enjoy, in consequence of his depriving another of his
life and liberty, *fully* to *overbalance* that
pain, which is the offspring of compassion,
what would then remain, to *restrain* him?

And as I am at present, in the inter-
rogatory humour of Socrates, I must beg
leave to ask further, WHAT CONSTITUTES
it MORE the RIGHT of ONE man, to enjoy
the pleasures, resulting from the LIFE and
LIBERTY, which nature gave him, than of
the OTHER, to enjoy the PLEASURE, which
results from the gratification of his DE-
SIRES; which, nature likewise gave him?
The question therefore, still remains unan-
swered. And indeed, could IT be *satisfac-
torily* answered, this is only a *leading* question, to *that*,—which is the precise one in
the instance, I have supposed, and quoted
from Mr. Locke. For in *that*, the SAME
MAN is in *two different cases*, in possession
of

of his *life* and *liberty*. In the one of which,
the man is conceived to have fuffered *no
hurt* from the other; in the other cafe,
he is fuppofed, to *have received one.* The
real queftion therefore is, and I beg you
will particularly obferve it, WHAT CON-
STITUTES HIS RIGHT to KEEP his life
and liberty, where he has done the other
NO HURT; and what CONSTITUTES the
RICHT of the *other*, to TAKE THEM AWAY,
where, he has?

For my own part, Sir, I have thought
long and much upon it; and can find
no leading idea, no feparating, nor con-
necting principle in the two cafes. And
as I am not prone, to *take* a propofition
for granted, becaufe, another man, whatever may be his reputation, affirms it;
I muft beg, as the condition, of my affent, even to a propofition of Mr. Locke's,
neither his, nor your WORDS; but either
your's, or fome other perfon's bond of

PROOF.

PROOF. I can however affure you, that in vain will you fearch for one, in the works of *Grotius, Puffendorf, Barbeyrac, Burlamaqui*, or, of any later writer upon government.

In vain likewife, will you, or even any fociety in this kingdom, however large in numbers, or dignified in rank and abilities, addrefs the NATIONAL ASSEMBLY of *France* for inftruction, upon this moft fundamental point. They, having already publifhed, in their *declaration of rights*,—all they know, upon this fubject; and which has with high encomiums, been more than once moft feduloufly diffeminated, throughout the kingdom. To thofe indeed, who love to walk in a mift, becaufe, the vapours, by confounding the outlines of things, ferve to magnify the objects; *their declaration* muft be moft highly, and moft gratefully acceptable. For do but attend once more, Sir, to what I do not doubt, you have often before

before read; I mean *this declaration of rights,*
which we are informed, holds out to the
world, " *inftruction, of great confequence to*
" *civil government,* and *founded upon* GREAT
" AUTHORITY, being agreed to by the NA-
" TIONAL ASSEMBLY of *France,* and *fanc-*
" *tioned* by the KING." I will only detain
you, by tranfcribing, TWO of thefe " *fimple*
" *and inconteftible principles,*" as they have
been called, and making a fhort comment
upon them, they having the moft intimate
connection with the queftion, now before
us, and befides having had the high honour, of being *felected,* to form a *bafis,* for
the reft.

" Men were BORN, and ALWAYS CON-
" TINUE FREE, and EQUAL, in refpect of
" their RIGHTS: civil diftinction THERE-
" FORE," *(which muft render men unfree,*
and *unequal)* " can be founded only on
" PUBLIC UTILITY," *(which is to fay there-*
fore in other words, that thefe natural rights
                                              of

of men, are incompatible with PUBLIC UTI-
·LITY.)

" The end of all POLITICAL affociations,
" IS the PRESERVATION of the NATURAL
" and IMPRESCRIPTIBLE RIGHTS of man ;"
*(which therefore according to the foregoing de-
claration; civil diſtinctions, for the fake of* PUB-
.LIC UTILITY, *take away)* and thofe RIGHTS,
are· LIBERTY, PROPERTY, SECURITY, and
RESISTANCE of OPPRESSION. *But all thefe
imprefcriptible rights. as they are called, the
very · inſtitution of government, and of laws,
is intended to* PRESCRIBE.

OH LEPIDUM CAPUT!

That the end, of all *political aſſociations,*
is to preferve to men, liberty, property,
fecurity, and refiftance of oppreffion, to a
certain degree, and not to deftroy them, as
the *national aſſembly* has done,—is indeed
true; and will be prefently proved. But,
this is,—by CONSTITUTING them to BE

I   the

the RIGHTS of men, under a ſtate of *go-vernment*, which, were NOT RIGHTS, in a *ſtate of nature*.

Theſe ſelf-taught legiſlators therefore you ſee, hold not out to you, the leaſt aſ-ſiſtance towards the ſolution of this almoſt *Sphinxian Ænigma*, with which you are puzzled. For the *national aſſembly, you* find, an aſſembly of *philoſophers*, undoubtedly as they are, have certainly adopted the eaſieſt, though not that, which either Plato, or Ariſtotle would have thought the *beſt* mode of inſtruction,—the taking,—I mean, a pro-poſition for granted,—inſtead of proving it.

Yet, ſo licentious are our public prints become, as to maintain, for I lately my-ſelf read the aſſertion in the news-papers, that the *framer* of this *luminous* DECLA-RATION, OF RIGHTS, is *undoubtedly* the WISEST MAN in FRANCE. Ought not ſuch calumniators to be puniſhed, for publiſhing

ſo

fo fcandalous a LIBEL on the UNDER-
STANDINGS, of THE WHOLE FRENCH
NATION.

Having now fpun out the thread of this
epiftle, as I truft, to a reafonable length,
and having propofed to you, a fubject beft
fitted for the retirement of your ftudy,
and the filence of meditation; it will I
apprehend, be moft proper, here to conclude this letter. For, would but the generality of authors, change their hours al-
lotted to reading and to thinking, into the
inverfe ratio of that, which they moft commonly bear to each other; the world
would foon be delivered from thofe great
evils,—great books. And ftudents then, at
once receiving the precious ore, pure and
defecated, would no longer either fweat
under the fatigue of clearing away the drofs,
or be covered, or choked with it's duft.

> I am, Sir,
> Yours, &c.

I 2   LETTER

L E T T E R IV.

Sir,

THOUGH I have often maintained, and
must always think, that how much
foever a man may BELIEVE, he can never
poffibly KNOW any thing, of which, he has
NEVER DOUBTED; yet as I am alfo perfuaded, that a conftant ftate of *fcepticifm*,
is the worft of all the chronic maladies,
which can afflict the human mind; I am
now eager to offer myfelf as your phyfici-
an, to deliver you from that irkfome ftate,
in which I left you, at the conclufion of
my laft letter. For, though fome portion,
or potion, of fcepticifm, is fometimes as
neceffary to keep the mind in a conftant

habit

habit of health and vigour, as a cathartic is fometimes beneficial to the body; yet, fcepticifm, which is, as it were, a mental diarrhœa, muft like the bodily one, infallibly end in debility, and diffolution. I hope however, this allufion will not give offence, either to your delicacy, or to the nice olfactory fenfes of others, in this refined age. Becaufe, I muft confefs, that 'till a new art of criticifm be written, I cannot difcover, either high or low, why mean allufions are not as properly fuited to low things; as the *loftieft* fimilitudes, are to the higheft fubjeEts.

Now Sir, though I can not poffibly attempt to fhow you, why LIFE and LIBERTY are more the NATURAL RIGHTS of MEN, than of HORSES, and where that intermediate *idea* exifts, which makes them fo, after which, we have been fo long enquiring, but have never found; yet I can very eafily find, and inform you of

the

the miftake, which led Mr. Locke into
this maze of error. A difcovery, certainly next in it's importance, to the difcovery of the object itfelf. Becaufe it will
fave . mankind in future, from the fruitlefs
labour, of darkly and ignorantly hunting
round and round, in fearch of an object, which has no exiftence; and the
difpute, upon NATURAL RIGHTS, will no
longer ofcillate, upon a mere fluctuating
argument ad ignorantiam; but, will be
fixed for ever, upon the immoveable point
of real fcience.

That *fome* men in a *ftate* of *nature*,
WOULD indeed take away another's life and
liberty, in ONE of the cafes fuppofed by
Mr. Locke, who would *not* do it in the
other; is a clear and indifputable fact.
But, that they would do this, without either knowing or thinking about NATURAL
RIGHTS, is infinitely more evident, than
any of his *axioms,* to which you fo readily

ly give your affent, and, which you deem
it criminal in others, to doubt.

For the NATURE of MAN is so CON-
STITUTED, that the paffions of ANGER,
HATRED, and REVENGE, naturally fpring
up in him, upon any attempt of another,
either to inflict upon him any pain, or to
deprive him of any pleafure, is likewife
certain beyond contradiction. But, if THESE
be the MOTIVES of HIS action, in the
cafe fuppofed, who has really SUFFERED
PAIN from another; then, he NO MORE
deprives that other of his LIFE and LI-
BERTY, from a SENSE of RIGHT, than
the OTHER, inflicted the PRIOR PAIN upon
THAT PRINCIPLE;—BOTH acting EQUAL-
LY from their paffions or appetites. The
one perhaps, to acquire a pleafure not
before poffeffed, the other to gratify revenge for a lofs fuftained.

No doubt, wife, is the provifion of nature, by which we are furnifhed with fuch

a

a paffion, as REVENGE, though the exercife of it, often brings great evils upon
mankind. But, equally wife likewife, is
that provifion, of nature, which furnifhes
us with other PASSIONS and DESIRES;
which produce alfo many evils, by urging
men to wifh for, and to attempt to take
away the poffeffions of others. But, so
FAR are the PASSIONS THEMSELVES, or
even the *refpective* STRENGTH of *different*
paffions, FROM CONSTITUTING a RIGHT
to THAT, which they prompt us to defire,
that in order for the very BIRTH and
ESTABLISHMENT of RIGHTS; RULES ·or
LAWS, are made to SUBDUE the ONE, and
to CONSTITUTE the other, which laws, are not
the offspring of PASSION, but of REASON.
And the PRINCIPLE which furnifhes men
with the power of reafoning upon this
point, and drawing out deductions, is the CON-
CLUSION, which experience has taught them,
from the endurance of paft evils, of. the
utility, and even NECESSITY there is, for
the

the inftitution of a government, and the eftablifhment of laws, fo as to conftitute it, the RIGHT OF a GOVERNOR, to PUNISH any one, who HURTS another; in order to PREVENT the actual EXERCISE of that VERY PASSION, by which, *Mr. Locke* fays, every man has a RIGHT to PUNISH another, and in confequence of which, the life of man had been, but one continued fcene of reciprocal infliction, and fuffering of wounds, pain, and death.

In a country indeed, where, the WILL of GOD had been made known to the inhabitants, directly by REVELATION, or where, by a revelation to one nation, fome knowledge of it had been transfufed to another by *tradition*, not only of the exiftence of a God, and fome religious worfhip or other,—which moft countries have;—but likewife, of HIS WILL, with regard to MEN'S CONDUCT to EACH OTHER, —of which, all people in a STATE OF

K   NATURE

NATURE, muſt have been always ignorant, without the ineſtimable benefit, either of ſuch a revelation, or ſuch a tradition,— THEY might indeed have CONCEIVED and TALKED of RIGHTS, and had a ground-work, upon which, they might have plead-ed them. But, if inſtead of imagining caſes, which never exiſted, but in ſome few particular inſtances, we have recourſe to true hiſtory, and real faſt,—we ſhall learn,—that the FIRST RIGHTS known to men, are thoſe, which had their origin, from *ſome ſpecies* of GOVERNMENT, however imperfeſt it might be; and it follows there-fore as a conſequence, that *government* is *not* founded upon PRIOR RIGHTS; but that IT only, aſtually by LAWS, delivered either orally, or in writing, CONVERTS THOSE POSSESSIONS INTO PROPERTY, and INTO RIGHTS; which, had before no OTHER TENURE, than that uncertain and precarious one, which was at all times, ſubjeſt to DISSOLUTION from the LUSTS,

APPETITES,

APPETITES, STRENGTH, VIOLENCE, and FORCE of OTHERS.

Harraſſed and fatigued, with ſo miſerable a ſtate of exiſtence, as this, o F NATURE, eſpecially, when men having forſaken the hunting and fiſhing ſtates, were brought into a nearer intercourſe with each other, by paſtoral, and agricultural occupations, they reſolved to terminate it, by ſearching out ſome remedy, againſt the continuance of theſe evils. This they effected, *firſt*, perhaps by providing a ſecurity againſt the external violence, they ſuſtained from other men, whoſe huts, or habitations, were at ſome diſtance from them; and who would frequently by ſurpriſe, in one night, extirpate, or enſlave, almoſt all the inhabitants of a wide extended diſtrict. *Secondly*, likewiſe, to guard themſelves from the equally bad conſequences, which aroſe from the more frequent evils, produced by the unreſtrained

K 2   exerciſe

exercife of the paffions, of thofe, who lived in a clofer vicinity with each other. From thefe flight fketches, the firft rude frame of a government was formed. Some by choice determining, and others, by neceffity being compelled, to fubmit to the government, or controul, of fome one man to direct them; who was either felected by others, or who having from fome caufe or other, acquired fuch authority amongft them, that they quietly fubmitted to his affumption of the rule, and command over them.

From thefe PREMISES, then, it NECESSARILY FOLLOWS, that the office of the governor, was, by uniting them in a body, to lead them out to war, to repel the attacks of diftant enemies; and by laying down laws, for the regulation of their conduct, and by the power of punifhment, intrufted in his hands,—to deter all the members of the feveral families, which by

their

their union, formed the state, from inter-
rupting each other, in the USE and PEACE-
ABLE ENJOYMENT, of their RESPECTIVE
ACQUISITIONS, except in such cases, as
the governor thought necessary for the
public good.

Such were the views, without doubt,
with which men associated together, and
such were the ends, which they proposed.

They, certainly did NOT unite into society, and form a government, for the
purpose of ACTING WITHOUT RESTRAINT,
according to the *volitions,* and *determinations*
of their own *passions, inclinations, caprice,*
or *fancy,* or even the CONCLUSIONS, OF
EACH MAN'S SEPARATE REASON. For on
the contrary, the very purpose of their
associating together, was to ESCAPE FROM
THE EVILS OF SUCH A STATE, where,
ALL WERE MISERABLE, FROM EACH MAN'S
ACTING ACCORDING TO HIS OWN WILL,
WITHOUT

WITHOUT THE CURB OF SOME COMMON CONTROUL. But, they united into fociety, and formed a GOVERNMENT, by giving authority TO ONE MAN, to PREVENT the EXERCISE OF SUCH FREE-WILL, and to PROVIDE SUCH A CONTROUL; by COMPELLING THEM to SUBMIT to fuch GENERAL LAWS, as HIS REASON fhould devife, and HIS POWER fhould enforce.

From the foregoing reafoning, then the CONCLUSION is EVIDENT;—that if any ONE, or any NUMBER of individuals, fet up (in fuch government as that, whofe formation I have been defcribing) HIS, or THEIR wills, in OPPOSITION to the WILL of the LEGISLATOR, HE or THEY are GUILTY of the GREATEST of ALL crimes, they can poffibly commit. Becaufe, it is a crime, which diffolves at once, the whole cement of fociety, and fnaps afunder by violence, all the bonds of government, which tend to fecure to the WHOLE,—

PEACE and TRANQUILITY. For OPPO-
SITION to the WILL of the LEGISLATOR,
tends to drive them back, to that MISE-
RABLE STATE OF NATURE, from which,
they gladly fled to GOVERNMENT, as to
a REFUGE and an ASYLUM. And hence
it was, that *Socrates*, who was efteemed
in Greece, as the wifeft of the fons of
men, however he may be now *defpifed* by
the *philofophers* of modern days, fubmitted
chearfully to die, in obedience to the laws, of
a *tyrannic republic*, as fuch there may be, however ftrange, fuch a notion may appear to
modern politicians. For notwithftanding *he*
was unjuftly condemned by his judges, he was
nobly inflexible to all the entreaties, and great
and generous pains, taken by his friends,
to perfuade him to efcape. To the honour of *Athens* however, it ought ever to
be remembered, that foon after his death,
the citizens were fincerely forry, and truly
penitent, for the injuftice and cruelty, with
which they had treated him; having been
feduced

seduced by the flimsy, but cruel misre-
presentations of a comic wit,—the mean
envy, or still meaner self-interest of elo-
quent sophists.—The contagious corruption
of a turbulent faction,—and the furious
phrenzy of a popular assembly.

It was then, from the *institution* of a
government, that there *first* arose in those,
who had not the WILL of GOD revealed
to them,—IDEAS of RIGHTS and WRONGS,
of OBLIGATION and DUTY, of MERIT and
DEMERIT, between men in *general*, who
were not bound to each other, by the ligaments of nature. By those *ligaments* I
mean, the *instincts*, and *affections* of the
mind, which reciprocally bind parents to
children,—husbands to wives,—brothers to
sisters,—friends to friends,—and in general,—
the person obliged to his benefactor. These
AFFECTIONS indeed, must in SOME DEGREE,
ALWAYS exist in every state of human
nature; whether they be, or be not under

any

any government; though, *even these feelings,* are very *faint* and *imperfect,* 'till the bridle by which government curbs our hostile desires, has subdued and broken the other unruly passions of our nature, taught men to move in certain regular and settled paces, and thus given an opportunity to the gentler and softer inclinations, to form themselves by HABIT,—INTO AFFECTIONS; which, were at first, —only EMOTIONS.

For it is surely very evident, that till some rules of action, in the manner I have stated, were prescribed,—there could be no MEASURE of the RECTITUDE, or DEVIATION of men's actions. For there could be no RIGHT in one man to ANY POSSESSION,—'till some *rule* had constituted it so, by forbidding and preventing others, from giving him any molestation in the enjoyment of it. There could be NO DUTIES, (except the reciprocal ones I have

before

before mentioned) 'till there was SOME OBLIGATION;—and there could be,—NO OBLIGATION, 'till,—there was SOME ONE, who had a POWER by fome motive, to OBLIGE another to do an act; and 'till there was another,—who was OBLIGED by that motive,—to OBEY. Men could be entitled to NO MERIT, nor DEMERIT from their conduct, 'till,—there was fome LAW, in confequence of which, they were by a NON-COMPLIANCE, with it, ENTITLED to BLAME, or fome OTHER PUNISHMENT; or which, by holding out REWARDS, as the confequence of a CONFORMITY with it, ENTITLED them to, or made them MERIT, or DESERVE praife, or fome other reward. Yet evident as fuch a conclufion, muft be to every mind, habituated to deep thought; what admired fyftems, of what is called, PHILOSOPHY have we feen, which place the exiftence of the ideas annexed to thefe words, for want of an accurate analyfis of their meaning, anterior,

terior, though certainly they are subfequent
to the formation of all laws, rules of
actions, rewards, and punifhments. And
thus it happens, that many a fair, fplendid, and beautiful fyftem, when the meaning of the words, which form the fundamental propofition of the whole fabric, are
fo examined as to be clearly afcertained,
tumble into pieces, and leaves it's fragments, as fome memorial of it's author's
genius, but, at the fame time, of his fruitlefs
labour, and his mifapplied application.

THESE are the PRINCIPLES then, from
which originates the RIGHT of the GO-
VERNOR to COMMAND; and, alfo the DUTY
of the GOVERNED to OBEY. To the former, in the cafe I have juft ftated, as
their LEGISLATOR, they have entrufted,
not only the POWER, but the RIGHT of
JUDGING for them, what actions each
man is to perform, fo as to act confiftently with the GENERAL GOOD of the whole.

And

And this too without any contract,—direct or implied,—any stipulation,—or condition of any RESISTANCE whatsoever, in any case whatsoever, when any number, few or many, the minority, or majority, should happen to think differently from the legislator, and not deem a law conducive to private, or public good. A trust which however LIABLE TO ABUSE, arose, from men's experience of the evils, which they sustained, whilst EACH individual acted according to the PRIVATE determination of his OWN WILL.

If therefore, the subjects attempt, by FORCE to defend themselves, from submission to the governor's authority, they certainly can not plead any RIGHT to do it, but are JUSTLY said,—to REBEL,—or to MAKE WAR again; and the governor, has consequently a RIGHT to SUBDUE them by a superior force, for invading HIS RIGHT, and every OTHER MAN'S RIGHT, as a member of the society.

For

For such a resistance, is an attempt to DISSOLVE and ANNIHILATE the GOVERNMENT itself; and to involve their fellow subjects once more, in all the ANARCHY, MISERY and CONFUSION, which attend upon A STATE OF NATURE. An attempt, which not only conſtitutes a FOLLY of the greateſt magnitude; but a CRIME likewiſe of the deepeſt dye. For, *that* one act of criminality, which tends to pluck up the whole happineſs, and exiſtence of the ſociety by the roots, muſt neceſſarily IMPLICATE in it's PERPETRATION, the UNITED FLAGITIOUSNESS OF EVERY OTHER CRIME.

If, the truth of theſe premiſes be denied, and I well know, that, on account of men's *prepoſſeſſions,* and *prejudices,* they will with the utmoſt difficulty be admitted; let *ſuch,* however reflect a moment upon the abſurdity, in which, they neceſſarily involve themſelves. For from the denial

of

of thefe principles, it will follow, that NO
INSTITUTION of GOVERNMENT can POS-
SIBLY SUBSIST. As the *very* DEFINITION
of the WORD, " GOVERNMENT," IMPLIES,
and confequently, the very ESSENCE of
the THING, MUST CONSIST, in the PEO-
PLE'S SUBMISSION, to the authority of
ONE or MORE PERSONS; as it's DIFFE-
RENT FORMS, may happen to VARY.
Which is the fame as to fay, in other
words,—that ALL the other members of the
community, are BOUND to SUBMIT to
HIS or THEIR JUDGMENT, as to what
general laws are to be made, to direct
each individual, what actions he is to perform, for the GOOD of the SOCIETY.

If then, the legiflature, *fhould enact* fuch
laws, as any number of them, even MUCH
MORE than the MAJORITY, may in their
own opinion, think have a direct contrary tendency; they can have no RIGHT,
nor LEGAL means of oppofing them, except

cept it may be by an humble reprefen-
tation, of their own opinions. But, if the
laws be not repealed in confequence of
fuch a petition, nothing is left to the pe-
titioners, but either quietly to acquiefce,
in the determination of the legiflature, or
to withdraw themfelves from that ftate, and
put themfelves under the protection of
another. For they, can not poffibly fet
forth any RIGHT whatfoever, on which,
they can build any CLAIM to OPPOSE the
laws by FORCE; becaufe, SUCH a CLAIM
would be a DEMOLITION *of the* WHOLE
COMPACT of fociety; which is,—that the
fubjects agreed to SUBMIT to the will and
JUDGMENT of the LEGISLATURE; NOT,
—that the GOVERNOR's and LEGISLATOR's
will, fhould fubmit to THEIRS.

As thefe principles, Sir, however mani-
feftly true, or evidently beautiful they may
be, in themfelves, or however good, and
wholefome may be their fruits, (for according

cording to the *platonic philofophy*, TRUTH, BEAUTY, and GOOD, are ONE) yet, as I am afraid, that they will notwithftanding, feem very *unpalatable* to you, I fhall by terminating this letter, once more leave you time, to chew upon them the cud of reflection.

I need not, I dare to fay, to affure you, that they will never be *clearly comprehended* by any one; 'till he has learned ACCURATELY to diftinguifh, between the *true* and *vulgar* application of WORDS to THINGS; and is able to place the IDEAS DIVESTED of THE WORDS, in their natural fhapes, colours and dimenfions, before the *orbit*, and *pupil* of his INTELLECT.

I am, Sir,

Yours, &c.

LETTER

LETTER V.

SIR,.

I Have now, given you an opportunity of taking what time you pleaſe, for concoƈting the FIRST PRINCIPLES OF ALL GOVERNMENT; if, *ſatiety* occaſioned by the diſhes, which *Mr. Locke* had ſerved up upon this occaſion, has not excited in you, ſuch an antipathy, as to produce an averſion even to *their* taſte.

Theſe principles, are certainly not faſhionable; and therefore not being popular, can not at preſent, be of any uſe to any

M   *artiſt,*

artift, in *book-making;* except, by the opportunity they afford of manufacturing fome
warcs for fale, in *oppofition* to them. For
when once an age is enlightened by the
fplendor of book-making, and has imbibed
it's genuine fpirit; the merit of a work
muft always be eftimated, according to
the valuation of Hudibras, who afks,

For what is worth in any thing?
then anfwers,

But fo much money as 'twill bring.

But whether you will with all the pertina-
city of bigotry, refolve to adhere to whatever
Mr. Locke has *told,*—for he certainly has
not *taught* it, you; either by a refufal of
further examination, and a maintenance of
it againft conviction; or, will begin to think
with Socrates, that there is no feafon of
a man's life, too late for the acquifition
of frefh knowledge, by exploring and
fearching after truth, to whatever diftance,
the inveftigation may lead;—is yours to
choofe,

choofe, not mine to dictate. But, if you be difpofed to make fuch an enquiry, that nothing may be omitted by me, which may at all tend to facilitate your progrefs:—I fhall beg leave, now, to remove TWO OB-JECTIONS;—which might perhaps otherwife, not only obftruct you in your road, but even, perhaps, prevent your acquifition, of the object of your purfuit.

For, you may poffibly imagine, in the FIRST place,—that, what I have affigned, as the VERY FIRST principles of ALL GO-VERNMENT, can at moft, be only the SE-CONDARY propofitions, founded upon *fome,* which were either *prior* to them in ex-iftence; or which, though pofterior, as to difcovery,—either fuperfede them by their importance, or deftroy them by their con-trariety.

SECONDLY, you may perhaps conceive, that however clear, and evident, the truth of

thofe

thofe PRINCIPLES, which I have advanced, appear to be; yet, they muft neceffarily be li-mited in their extent, to a *certain degree*. For you will probably urge, that if we trace out the conclufions, which *unavoidably* follow from them,—it is neceffary,—that we fhould *rejeɛt* the *principles*, in their *utmoft latitude;* from fear, of the . danger, which would refult from their CONSEQUENCES. As you will perhaps, under this *fecond head*, affert, that upon thefe principles,—OBEDIENCE, is as much · due to the WORST, as to the BEST government in the world,—which, YOU will *deem* to be abfurd: and that the cruelleft aɛts, of the moft DESPOTIC TYRANT, are to be by them JUSTIFIED, upon the ground of RIGHT;—which you will juftly condemn as IMMORAL.

As to the FORMER OBJECTION, it is certainly founded upon PROPOSITIONS, which, have occafioned all the difficulty, confufion,

confufion, and perplexity, in which the
NATURE of government, has been hitherto
involved; and which have veiled it in
the thickeft mift of cimmerian darknefs.

But, upon an attentive examination, it
will be found, that the objeftion is wholly grounded upon an error, which,—though
very common,—is,—yet fo grofs;—as that,
—of MISTAKING,—an EFFECT,—for it's
CAUSE.

Clearly and fully however, to demon-
ftrate this, I muft beg leave, to trace out
the ORIGIN and foundation of ALL MO-
RAL PRINCIPLES.

A fubjeft, upon which, I apprehend my
opinions will be thought, to differ more
from thofe of *former* writers, than any
pofition which has hitherto been advanced,
upon the FIRST PRINCIPLES of government. Notwithftanding therefore, *both* have
the

the moſt indiſſoluble connection, and are inſeparably interwoven with each other, I muſt entreat you, Sir, and every one elſe; who *really wiſhes* to UNDERSTAND, the REASONING and CONCLUSIONS under that head, to vouchſafe me, the cooleſt, and moſt unprejudiced attention.

In the FIRST PLACE, I might, I apprehend, take for granted,—which is an act I am not in the habit of doing, that there are no INNATE IDEAS, and conſequently, —no INNATE MORAL PRINCIPLES, or NOTIONS;—ſuch as thoſe, I mean, which were formerly maintained. An opinion, which I doubt not, *you* will allow, has been properly exploded, being faſhioned, only, of "*ſuch ſtuff as our dreams are made of.*"

SECONDLY, that the word, CON- SCIENCE, ſignifies only, the INTERNAL AP- PROBATION, and DISAPPROBATION, of which, we feel *ourſelves* to be the *objects*, either as we perform certain actions, or omit

the

the performance of them, and vice verſa; but, that it DOES NOT imply alſo the RULE of ACTION ITSELF; which, at the time, we either conform to,—or tranſgreſs. Since, we muſt aſſuredly, have *firſt known* the *rule*, and learned, that, it was WORTHY of approbation, or diſapprobation, before we could feel ourſelves DESERVING, or, UNDESERVING of THOSE SENSATIONS.

But leſt you or any other of my readers, ſhould refuſe to admit, theſe PROPOSITIONS as TRUTHS, take the following, " *reductio ad abſurdum:*" which is equally applicable to *every ſpecies* of ſuppoſition,— of *innate ideas,—innate notions,*—and of a MORAL SENSE. For from the admiſſion of *any one* of them, then it would follow, —that ALL the RULES and PRACTICES, in *different* ſocieties, would be guided by ONE UNIFORM INSTINCT; and the SAME ACTIONS of conduct, would be INVARIABLY, and UNIVERSALLY APPROVED in

ALL

ALL the various countries, nations, and tribes upon earth. Which, is a circumſtance, we know to be REPUGNANT, to ALL the documents of hiſtory, and ALL the concluſions of experience.

From theſe DATA, then it neceſſarily follows, that the RULES of MORAL SCIENCE, muſt be deduced, as ALL OTHER SCIENCES ARE, from the INDUCTION of PARTICULAR FACTS; from which, are formed GENERAL PROPOSITIONS. But, as the SCIENCE of MORALS, or a SYSTEM of VIRTUE, is invented, to teach men, to regulate their behaviour to each other, UNIVERSALLY; NO SUCH SCIENCE, could POSSIBLY EXIST, 'TILL SOME PARTICULAR RULES had FIRST been layed down for THIS PURPOSE; as, THAT SCIENCE, muſt CONSIST LIKE ALL OTHERS, in GENERALISING PARTICULAR RULES. Hence then it likewiſe follows, that an UNION, muſt firſt have been formed amongſt mankind,

kind, and *particular rules* muſt have been tried, before, the GENERAL rules could have been FRAMED. Becauſe, as the *general* rules *conſtitute* the *ſcience*, and THESE muſt have been GENERALISED out of PARTI-CULAR rules, the LAST, muſt have been PRIOR, to the SCIENCE ITSELF.

From theſe premiſes then, the ORIGIN and PROGRESS of MORAL SCIENCE, clearly, and manifeſtly flow. For, in conſequence of the FREEDOM, LEISURE, and SECURITY, which men enjoy under the protection of any tolerably well regulated government, be it's form, what it will; the wants of men increaſing with increaſing numbers, impel men's minds to the diſcovery of the MEANS, beſt ſuited, to a conſtant ſupply of their gratifications. Hence, *firſt* ariſe, ſome of the more immediately uſeful, but moſt obvious arts and ſciences. But as by exerciſe, men's attention and faculty of reaſon, gradually ſtrengthen, and improve,

N they

they advance in the difcovery of others, certainly not lefs ufeful, but more abftrufe. From much exercife in determining, the *quantum* of good, which refults from one particular MODE of ACTING, in a prefent and particular cafe, they proceed to frame GENERAL PROPOSITIONS and PRINCIPLES, upon ALL fubjects; and to have a habit of forefight and fagacity; by which, they are enabled to penetrate into remote confequences; and to form comparifons, between very diftant objects. Hence then, having obferved, that the GRAND END, for which men united into fociety, was to fecure the GENERAL HAPPINESS of every order, rank, and fituation; and that the MEANS to this, was by their UNIVERSAL OBEDIENCE to the WILL of their LEGISLATOR, who was appointed to CURB and RESTRAIN by LAWS, the inclinations and paffions of thofe, who would otherwife act contrary to that principle;—they foon learned to ABSTRACT from their PARTICULAR ftate and fituation, all thofe GE-

NERAL

NERAL RULES, by which their actions are regulated, and to conceive them to be EQUALLY BINDING upon ALL mankind, in every place, whether, they do, or do not exift, as the LAWS of their PARTICULAR STATE. When they have advanced, *thus far*, then,—thofe who act according to thofe *univerfal principles*, without any reference to the punifhments, which the *law* of the *ftate* inflicts,—they call,—VIRTUOUS;—and they who deviate from them,—they term, —VICIOUS; in *contradiftinction* to thofe, who only obeying, or difobeying the *laws* of their particular government,—*as being* the *laws* of their government,—are denominated HONEST, or DISHONEST,—JUST or UNJUST.

Again, after men have turned their refearches to the *nature* of *man*, and of the *human mind*, and deduced fome *general* principles, from fuch an enquiry,—they begin to afpire after the acquifition, of

fome

fome knowledge,—of the DIVINE MIND,
or of the NATURE of GOD. Some inti-
mation of WHOSE EXISTENCE, and fome
fcanty notion of HIS nature,—of his being
the DIVINE LEGISLATOR, or rewarder and
punifher of man,—they had perhaps before
reaped from fome *immediate* or *remote* TRA-
DITION. Impelled then by this curiofity,
and affifted, by this information, they be-
gan to endcavour to DEMONSTRATE, HIS
EXISTENCE, from the DEDUCTIONS, of
their own REASON. For, we invariably
find, in ALL the PROOFS, in ALL nations,
which are given of the EXISTENCE of a
GOD, the FIRST ALWAYS is,—the *general*,
—or as it is commonly, but not juftly
called, the UNIVERSAL BELIEF of · that
notion, in *other* countries.

As fcience of all kinds advanced, and
men attained to a more intimate knowledge of the WORKS of NATURE in *particular*,—they learned,—that THESE, are ALL
generally

generally conducive to the HAPPINESS of mankind; and finding, that *human* governments, which originated from the REASON of MAN, directly tended to the SAME END; —they concluded, that he who would *always* act upon *that* principle, would approach neareſt, and be moſt acceptable to God; and therefore inferred,—that a DIVINE GOVERNMENT,—muſt have been eſtabliſhed by the WISDOM of GOD,—*conducive* alſo to the SAME END; in conſequence of which, he would inflict puniſhments upon the vicious, and diſpenſe rewards to the virtuous.

SUCH is the SOURCE,—from whence,— ſpring the LAWS of VIRTUE, and every PRINCIPLE, whether right or wrong,—of what is called,—MORALITY, and NATURAL RELIGION. And indeed, much OBSERVATION, muſt have been made upon the WORKS of NATURE, ſo as to diſcern, that whatever *ſubordinate* agents might be *employed,*

ployed,—yet, ONE UNCONTROULABLE WILL, directed the WHOLE, and the *faculties* of the *human mind* alfo, muft have received a *confiderable degree* of *cultivation*,—before, —*thofe men*,—who had received *no immediate* REVELATION from HEAVEN,—or *certain tradition* of one, — could poffibly have ceafed to be POLY.THEISTS; notwithftanding the information, which, a *primæval tradition*, might have faintly, though *generally* diffufed.

But *Socrates*, and *Plato*, having moft deeply inveftigated, both the lower and the higher powers, and faculties of the *human mind*,—and by a moft laborious cultivation of the faculty of INTELLECT, to a degree I may fay with truth, FAR BEYOND that, to which the *moderns* have *yet arrived*,— clearly difcerning the DIFFERENCE, and even OPPOSITION between MIND and BODY;—maintained,—that GOD would reward and punifh men, in *another life*, in pro-

portion

portion to their virtue or vice here; and as the *neceſſary foundation* to this doctrine, —attempted to raiſe it, upon a DEMON-STRATION of the NATURAL IMMORALITY of the HUMAN SOUL.

But, as the moſt elevated human in-tellect, CAN only be able to DEMONSTRATE, — that there is NO NECESSARY CON-NECTION,—between the DISSOLUTION of the BODY, and the *conſequent* ANNIHI-LATION of the SOUL,—and can only ſhow, merely from PROBABLE arguments, drawn from the GENERIC DIVERSITIES in the NATURES of both,—and likewiſe, from our *faint conception* of the WISDOM and GOOD-NESS of GOD,—that *ſuch* a ſurvival of the ſoul, ſeems a *neceſſary mean* to the pro-greſs of virtue here, and it's reward here-after,—the queſtion,—as to the minds *actual ſurvival,* was by the very NATURE of the EVIDENCE, *neceſſarily* involved (to the *ge-nerality* of the world) in much DOUBT, —great DIFFICULTY,—and no little per-plexity.

plexity. Though certainly, to thofe, who
are capable of following thefe almoft divine
philofophers in their fpeculations, through
the knowledge of the nature of MIND,
which *they* difcovered,—muft confefs,—that
THEY raifed the fuppofition, that God
has conftituted the HUMAN MIND, for
a CONTINUANCE of EXISTENCE, *after*
the diffolution of the body,—to the very
higheft fummit of proof, to which,—the
nature of *that* fpecies of evidence,—can
POSSIBLY afcend. But, as the queftion,
after which, they enquired,—was neceffarily a queftion of FACT,—it could not
POSSIBLY be ASCERTAINED by REASON-
ING,—but only,—as all other facts muft
be,—either,—by our own actual EXPERI-
ENCE,—or, the TESTIMONY of others.
Reafoning being of no further ufe, even
in inftituting experiments, relative to the
objects of our fenfes,—than the *contrivan-
ces* of *means*,—to render fome things *fenfible*, which were before unperceived. But
as in this life, we certainly can never
EXPERIENCE, what is the will and IN-

TENTION of God, in refpect to another,
—they CANNOT POSSIBLY therefore, be
MADE KNOWN to us, but by the TESTI-
MONY OF SOME ONE,—who produces the
AUTHORITY of GOD TO RÉVEAL THEM.

It muft likewife be confeffed, much as
I admire and reverence the *Socraticos Viros,*
as *Tully* fome where calls them, that their
fuppofition (though I know not that any
one has before obferved it in, *this* fenfe)
was calculated, only in a manner, for *philofophers.* As in the *focratic philofophy,* virtue
is fynonimous with wifdom, to which the
vulgar could not afpire; and VICE. with
IGNORANCE; in which they were neceffarily involved. Not becaufe philofophers,
who difcovered it, could not have in-
ftructed them in virtue, as *Sherlock,* (who
was however one of the deepeft thinkers,
and clofeft reafoners of this age, too much
fo, for the generality of readers to un-
derftand) has fuppofed. For *they* might
Q have

have been taught, VIRTUE as an ART,—
as they are taught OTHER arts, without
UNDERSTANDING the PRINCIPLES, which
are the CONCLUSIONS of SCIENCE; but
the real reason was, because no HUMAN
TEACHER'S AUTHORITY, supplied a sufficient MOTIVE, to induce them to learn
it, or urge them to practice it, if learned.*

These enquiries, whose speculations were
comprehended under the name of PHILO-
SOPHY, when they were once begun, excited much attention, in the ablest, and
most enlightened minds; and continued to
give

* There are animals, we know, who prefer
thistles, nettles, thorns, and briers, to the finest
grass, of the richest pastures. Similar to theirs,
seem to be the tastes of those who prefer, the
weedy works of some other English divines, to
the firm, and nourishing productions, raised by
the genius of a *Sherlock*.

give exercife, to much acutenefs of reafoning, and much fubtilty of difpute. From
hence arofe therefore, a variety of diffenfions, and divifions, not only amongft
the *antients*, but likewife amongft the *moderns*, as they happened to be more or
lefs prepoffeffed in favour of one, or other
of the different Grecian philosóphers,
from whofe fpeculations, fuch notions are
chiefly derived, and propagated.

For, the difciples of *Socrates*, (excepting
thofe who followed *Plato*) foon feparated
into various fects, and were divided by a
multitude of opinions. And, not being able to
fatisfy themfelves in the demonstration
of a future exiftence, *again* abstracted
the laws of *virtue* from the will, and
authority of a legislature, and the
fanctions of future rewards and punifhments. But then turning their enquiries to
the summum bonum, or what conftitutes

O 2   the

the higheſt happineſs of this life; each, endeavoured to find out SOME PRINCIPLE, . which . would make VIRTUE, and the SUMMUM BONUM to be ONE.

Some, as the STOICS, maintained that, VIRTUE, was indiſputably the SUMMUM BONUM, becauſe, the WISE and VIRTUOUS MAN, was *incapable* of ALL SUFFERING; as even PAIN, was to HIM, NO EVIL. For as HE, according to their maxims, muſt,—before he was entitled to thoſe appellations,—have learned to DESIRE nothing, but what HAPPENS·to him; therefore it followed,—that no condition, nor event, could befall him,—but, what HE approved. A doɛtrine evidently true indeed, upon the PRINCIPLES of CHRISTIANITY; where, pain is *really no evil;* —becauſe it is neceſſary to lead man to ſeek, as the firſt objeɛt of his purſuit,— his FUTURE FELICITY. From whence it foilows, as a corollary, that no event, can

possibly

I

poffibly happen to the real CHRISTIAN, which will not *conduce* to his *good*, if we take into our view, the whole extent of his being. But, upon any other fuppo-fition, this ftoical doctrine is perfectly ri-diculous. Becaufe it raifes a fuperftructure, without a foundation,—which the mere preffure, even of a fingle ftone, is at once able to deftroy.

Some, with EPICURUS himfelf, for moft of his difciples mifreprefented their mafter, founded the practice of it, upon the con-ftant *eafe* and *pleafure*, or rather, *tranqui-lity* of mind, which virtue affords. An opinion, which, if this world *only* be con-fidered, every day's experience contradicts.

Some again with the PERIPATETICS, ac-knowledged that *outward objects*, afforded pain and pleafure, and that though virtue therefore, did not produce the *only* fatisfacti-on, yet, upon the *whole*, it afforded the GREAT-

EST

EST pleasure. But this system, by authorising such a contrariety of pursuits, as
ACKNOWLEDGED MEANS to HAPPINESS,
carries in it's own frame, the seeds of it's
own destruction.

Others again with CICERO, who in his OF-
FICES adopted, only a part of Plato's doctrine,
or rather still more closely followed Panetius,
founded VIRTUE on the HONESTUM, or
the HONOURABLE; i. e. on the APPRO-
BATION of mankind. A theory, which
must shake with every blast. As, FAME
for VIRTUE, no more than for SCIENCE,
is, by any means distributed in proportion,
to REAL MERIT. For, few men, can penetrate into the deep recesses of the heart,
where only it can be accurately discerned;
and therefore, the artful, cunning, design-
ing hypocrite, is often puffed into renown,
by the public breath; whilst, the wisest
and the best, are frequently exposed to all
the

the blasts of envy,—and all the whispers of malignity.

But at length, GOD having been pleased to REVEAL HIS WILL to ALL mankind, both,—in respect to the AFFECTIONS, which are required from man,—the RULE OF CONDUCT he is to pursue; and the REWARDS or PUNISHMENTS,—which are to attend upon his obedience or disobedience; men have now *abstracted* STILL BETTER PRINCIPLES, from the DECLARATIONS of the GREAT AUTHOR, and formed them into systems, either of what they call VIRTUE,—or of what they call MORALITY,—or NATURAL LAW,—or NATURAL RELIGION. Hence, MANY have been induced to suppose, that because these are *consonant* with the *principles of* the CHRISTIAN RELIGION, *that religion* has revealed to us, *no other rules* of conduct, than what our own *natural reason* could discover; and notwithstanding therefore, they
admit

admit the *rules*, they reject the *authority*, upon which they are built; and even ridicule the *evidence*, by which, they are established.

Mankind then, having totally forgotten, or, having never learned, what *experience* could have taught them, of the procefs of the human mind, in the difcovery · of all the duties, which proceed from the exercife of their own faculties; and what, with all their application, they were incapable of difcovering; whatever RIGHT or DUTY,—however difcovered, which *appears* to them to be REASONABLE, they conclude, to have been the produce of that faculty, from it's earlieft cultivation. Involved in this miftake, they produce fyftems, as containing ORIGINAL, ETERNAL, and IMMUTABLE OBLIGATIONS, by which they affert, that ALL MEN were EVER bound to act, BEFORE the EXISTENCE of ANY GOVERNMENT; i. e. even before

there

there was the *poffibility* of the purfuit of any *invefligations*, which are the ONLY MEANS to *that* END. Thofe then, who are once feduced into thefe errors, confequently confider, the above really *diftinct*, and *feveral feparate* SPECIES of knowledge, as having only ONE SIMPLE INVARIABLE caufe; and that caufe, as being the SOLE ORIGIN of ALL men's VARIOUS RIGHTS, and DUTIES WHATSOEVER. Whereas, on the contrary, SO FAR, AS ANY of them, were DISCOVERED by MEN, they were only the DEDUCTIONS,—which they had made, in CONSEQUENCE of the RIGHTS, to which, GOVERNMENT FIRST GAVE BIRTH; and muft therefore, be SUBSEQUENT, NOT PREVIOUS to IT's EXISTENCE.

So likewife, fuch a fyftem of doctrines as the CHRISTIAN REVELATION contains, could not have been attended with any benefit to mankind, *(except* to *thofe,* to

P   whom

whom it was given as a *completion* of a *former)* 'till the eftablifhment of *human governments* and *laws*, and the *tradition* of the EXISTENCE of a GOD,—had led men into fpeculations, and enquiries, concerning WHAT actions, were moft probably pleafing to, that FIRST CAUSE, and PRE- SERVER of ALL THINGS. *This,* we may learn from *experience* of objects, which, if we do not actually fee, are however made known to us in the pages of hiftory. For, from it's records we learn; that there are now *many nations,* though they may be taught to believe, in the *authenticity* of the *chriftian religion,* are, for want of the exercife, of their reafon on civilization, and other arts, totally unfitted for the *practice* of it's *duties.** And on the con- trary, all thofe in the moft cultivated na- tions,

---

* See my COMMENCEMENT *Sermon,* before the *Univerfity* of Cambridge.

tions, who CONCEIVE *thofe duties* to be NO OTHER, than what are DISCOVERABLE by REASON;—are incapable of embracing, and relifhing, the *pureft* and *fublimeft*, of it's doctrines. For they even deem *that*, to be MORAL *conduct*, which originates only in the NATURAL PASSIONS of mankind, —fuch as VANITY,—PRIDE,—AMBITION, and REVENGE.

Thus, as *fome* in their theory, do not difcriminate the *various origins* of thefe fyftems, fo *others* in their practice, confound their *different effects*. From whence it proceeds, that the SAME OUTWARD ACT, which is often done from VARIOUS MOTIVES, is in common language, in ALL thefe CASES, equally termed, GOOD, and VIRTUOUS. Whereas, upon the *principles* of *chriftianity*, it is NOT the OUTWARD FORM,—but ONLY the MOTIVE,—which conftitutes an act *virtuous*, or *vicious*. And therefore, *many may do*, what in common

difcourfe,

difcourfe, are called *good actions,*—becaufe, in·their *confequences,* they are *attended* with *good* to others;—who are, by no means *really* entitled, to the denomination of GOOD MEN.

' Whatever *fyftem* of MORAL DUTY however, be felected; and whatever be the *motive* chofen as the incentive, to urge us to correfpondent actions; *not one* of them, have the *leaft tendency* to ALTER the RE-·LATION, between the GOVERNOR and the GOVERNED; as to the RIGHT of COM-·MAND in the one, and of the DUTY of OBEDIENCE in the other. And, if the TRU-EST, and SUREST principles be chofen, which are likewife fanctioned by the STRONGEST MOTIVES, and of whofe UNERRING REC-TITUDE, there can be no doubt,—as they come from GOD's WISDOM, NOT MAN's REASON; THEY have, certainly at leaft an *immediate* tendency, not only to *mollify,* and even to *fubdue,* all thofe paffions

of

of PRIDE, AMBITION, AVARICE, and. RE-
VENGE; which are, equally the CAUSES,
of TYRANNY in the SOVEREIGN, and of
RESISTANCE in the SUBJECT. THEY therefore, not only,—*teach*, but command the
former, NOT to inflict any pain or penalty, but what is *absolutely* neceſſary, to the
PUBLIC GOOD; not indeed, under the
penalty of their SUBJECT'S REBELLION,
but of GOD'S PUNISHMENT. But, they
likewiſe *inſtruct*, and *enable* the LATTER,
by the moſt forcible injunctions, and the
brighteſt examples of CHRIST, and his
APOSTLES, where the GOVERNOR,—even
NEGLECTS HIS DUTY,—to SUBMIT with
PATIENCE, not only, " for WRATH, but
" likewiſe,—for CONSCIENCE ſake."

And here, Sir, I can not forbear to
obſerve, that as FALSE PHILOSOPHY, is
continually receding farther, and farther,
from CHRISTIANITY; ſo the TRUE, ap-
proximates as near to it, as *finite*, can, to
infinite

infinite wifdom. For, I have before fug-
gefted to you, the *example* of *Socrates*, in
HIS *obedience*, to the fentence of his un-
juft judges. And could I, but prevail upon
you, to read only *Plato's little dialogue*,
between Socrates and Crito, and attentively
to ftudy, and digeft it, it would perhaps
impart to you infinitely more real benefit,
than you ever received from *all* the volumes upon government, you have *formerly
read*, or even the ESSAY, upon *that fubject*, (as you call it) which you have *long
fince written*, and I *long fince refuted*. For
then,

Hi motus animorum, atque hœc *certamina tanta,*
Pulveris exigui jactu, compreffa *quiefcant.*

If I fail in this appeal, to the FASCI-
NATING NAME of PHILOSOPHY, the GRAND
DIRECTRESS of MODERN TIMES; the *now*
GUARDIAN

GUARDIAN PATRONESS of *France*, though *their* philofophy is indeed totally different from *that*, I have juft now recommended, —I defpair of any efficacy,—from the *paffages*, to which I have alfo, juft now *referred* you, in the *pages* of CHRISTIA-NITY; perfpicuous as are their words, and confequently, evident as is their fenfe.

With *fuch wonderful* plainnefs indeed, do they inculcate, both by *precept* and *ex-ample*, the DUTY of SUBJECTS to their RULERS, that one would think, it is ac-tually impoffible, for *every one*, who has not drank to the very dregs of MODERN PHILOSOPHY, and who really believes, in the TRUTH of the CHRISTIAN RELIGION, to WITHOLD his ASSENT from the DE-CLARATION, or to REFUSE his OBEDI-ENCE to the INJUNCTION. How mortify-ing foever it may be to fome, to withdraw their allegiance from *modern philofophers*, in fubmiffion to the higher *authority* of

CHRIST;

CHRIST; yet, if they *do acknowledge*, the *authority* of the *laſt*, to be ſuperior, to that of the *former*, they muſt comply, and acknowledge, obedience in ſubjects, is due to their rulers, WHETHER THEY BE MILD and GENTLE, or CRUEL and TYRANNI-CAL :—Even impoſſible, as it appears to *ſome* of *your* admirers and ſcholars,—that ſuch a *declaration*, and *acknowledgment*,—ſhould be made by ANY ONE, in the concluſion, of this MOST ENLIGHTENED, EIGHTEENTH, CENTURY.

Nay, Sir, ſuch likewiſe, muſt neceſſari-ly have been the predicament, in which, even YOU YOURSELF, would have ſtood, had it not been, for that moſt HAPPY, and moſt WONDERFUL DISCOVERY, of a RATIONAL RELIGION; whoſe AUTHORITY, outweighs, the *authenticity* of REVELATION. A diſcovery, which ſome of the bigots of our eſtabliſhment, are too deſtitute of abi-lities, to comprehend. For they are ſo

weak

weak as to conceive, that the words "RA-
"TIONAL RELIGION," and the RELIGION
of REASON,—muſt be *ſynonimous*. But, as
ſuch an imagination betrays, as you well
know, the blindeſt ignorance;—I do not
wonder, that we always ſee YOU,—your
admirers and *followers*,—loſe your *meekneſs*,
—your *patience*,—and your *temper*,—whenever you have occaſion to mention the
ARTICLES, DOCTRINES, or MINISTERS of
the *Church* of *England*.

For if the above ſtupid ſuppoſition, of ſome
of the members of that *worſt* of all churches,
for ſuch I am told, it is, in your writings,
—were true,—then, the *groſſeſt* of all *ab-
ſurdities*, would follow,—viz.—that the CHRIS-
TIAN REVELATION, and RATIONAL RE-
LIGION, would be REALLY ONE, and, THE
SAME THING. Becauſe, when once a RE-
VELATION IS GIVEN to ALL MANKIND,—
THAT ALONE,—muſt be the only RATIONAL
RELIGION;—IF it be REASONABLE, that

Q   the

the CONJECTURES of MAN'S REASON,—
ſhould SUBMIT to the DECLARATIONS of
DIVINE WISDOM.

Whereas in faƈt, nothing can be more
DIRECTLY OPPOSITE to *each other*, than
GOD'S REVELATION, and what, YOU, call,
RATIONAL RELIGION. The *latter* being a
diſpenſation only to ſome CHOSEN FEW,
to enable them to determine, by the ſuperior light of their faculties, but from
the exerciſe of which we find, by experience, every received rule of LOGIC, muſt
firſt be *diſcarded*,—what PARTS of GOD's
REVELATION they are *pleaſed* to *admit*,
and what they *chuſe* to *rejeƈt*. Preciſely
in the ſame manner, as we find, has
likewiſe been imparted to them, the RIGHT
of CHUSING, what laws of the legiſlature
they will obey, and what, they will vilify
and abuſe. So intimately conneƈted, are
your RELIGIOUS, and POLITICAL PRIN-
CIPLES, and ſo cloſe is the ALLIANCE,
which

which you conceive to exift, between RE-
LIGION and CIVIL GOVERNMENT; and
confequently therefore, between CIVIL and
RELIGIOUS ESTABLISHMENTS.

There may be fome, Sir, perhaps, fo
ignorant, but I take for granted then,
they can only be amongft my brother
minifters of the eftablifhment, who, according to your repeated declarations, and
thofe of your friends, are the MOST IGNO-
RANT of all divines; as to fancy,—SUCH a
RATIONAL RELIGION, muft neceffarily be
the offspring only of pride, vanity, and arrogance, becaufe, they imagine, that it's APOS-
TLES, and their converts, muft conceive
THEMSELVES to be WISER, than HE, who
PROVED his AUTHORITY, to REVEAL the
WILL of GOD. But if men, who are dull
enough to make fuch a fuppofition, were
capable of reading an author, who though
he was not of your fect, was admirably
well acquainted with your doctrines;—they

Q 2 might

might learn,—that this claim to RATIONAL RELIGION, is one of the NATÚRAL IM-PRESCRIPTIBLE RIGHTS of your PERSUA-SION. For this author, I mean the *learn-ed Butler*, tells us,

Suppofe the Scriptures are of *force*,
They're but *commiffions* of courfe,
And *Saints* have *freedom* to digrefs,
And *vary from them* as *they pleafe.*

Having thus accompanied you, to take a view of the foundation of the ONLY PRINCIPLES, which can enable you to REJECT, the otherwife DECISIVE and IR-RESISTIBLE determination of REVELATION upon *this* fubject; I will, by concluding this letter,—leave you to the pleafing con-folation it affords.

And am, Sir,

Yours, &c.

LETTER

LETTER VI.

SIR,

HAVING already vindicated the ORIGIN of thofe principles, which I have affigned above,—againſt the impu- tation of ERROR; I am now likewife to defend the CONSEQUENCES,—which refult from them,—againſt the accufation of AB- SURDITY, and INJUSTICE.

To thofe,—who having not the benefit of thofe principles, with which the fore- going letter concludes, and by which, men

are

are enabled to fhelter themfelves, even from the CONVICTION, which REVELA-TION is fitted to impart, I doubt not, but I fhall be able to defend the principles I have advanced, as clearly againft the objection to their *confequences*, as againft the other to their *origin*.

Each objection, may perhaps upon a hafty and fuperficial view, appear to be as weighty and valuable as gold. But when both are put into the oppofite fcale, to be tried with it, they will both be found in the balance of truth, totally de-ficient in their fpecific gravities, and con-fequently of no intrinfic value.

For, *firft*, I not only moft readily grant, that *no tyranny* or *cruelty* in a governor, can poffibly be JUSTIFIED; fo likewife I maintain, that the PRINCIPLES, which I have advanced, have not the remoteft tendency, towards any attempt, at it's juftification ;—

but

but on the contrary, that they in the ſtrongeſt manner pronounce their condemnation. ·

I admit indeed, that from ·thoſe PRIN-CIPLES, it follows, that UNIVERSAL OBEDIENCE to the government, of what-ever nature it be, whether it be admi-niſtered by the uncontrouled WILL of ONE MAN, of a FEW, or of MANY;— or it be ſhared in any proportions, between ONE, a FEW, and MANY,—is EQUALIY, the DUTY of the *governed.* And, however the propoſition, when thus *plainly* and *un-equivocally* ſtated, may appear to *ſome;* yet certainly, it is not only VIRTUALLY, but alſo POSITIVELY admitted by ALL, who allow, that an ABSOLUTE UNCONTROULA-BLE POWER, muſt exiſt SOMEWHERE, in EVERY STATE. For, amongſt all the airy viſions, and meteorous coruſcations, which are continually gliding through the politi-cal atmoſphere, of this floating Iſland;— THIS POSITION, has never, within the ſphere of my remembrance, been denied.

It being as self-evident, at least as any proposition can be, that without *such* an ·ABSOLUTE power, not only, no constitution could be of any *long duration*, but that it could not even for a moment, *subsist*.

For, if a government was even so absurdly constituted, that the PEOPLE were under NO OBLIGATION to OBEY a law, 'TILL,—it had been PROPOSED to EVERY *district, city, town,* *village,* and *parish,* of a wide extended empire, and had been APPROVED,—by the MAJORITY of ALL the inhabitants,—*men, women,* and *children,*— THIS would not in the *smallest degree* INVALIDATE my CONCLUSION. Nay, the position would remain *equally true,* were even, *so absurd,* a constitution of government to exist,—as the following,—which is perhaps still *more* absurd, than the foregoing ;—viz. that the *majority* of the *people,* —*men,*—*women,*—and *children,* (and what could the most ardent lovers of LIBERTY and REPUBLICANISM *wish* for *more)* should

in *every diftrict, city, town, village,* and *parifh,*
have a RIGHT to RESIST every law, which
they do not approve, the very *firft time,*
it was *attempted* to be *executed, after* it had
been paffed; and it is to *one* or *other* of
thefe ABSURDITIES, ALL the plans of politicians in this *enlightened age,* ULTIMATE-
LY TEND. For even then, there MUST
be an UNCONTROULABLE ABSOLUTE POW-
ER, *fomewhere* EXISTING in the STATE,
notwithftanding the legiflative power chief- -
ly refided (as no doubt it ought) in the
very *dregs* of the people, (as they have been
inadvertently called by fome, who have the
profoundeft veneration for their judgment,)
and who in that cafe, would indeed be
the *enlightened legiflators* of *fuch* a conftitution. But I fay, that even then, for
fear, that the people,—*after* they had *once*
given their confent to a law, which had
been paffed, for which, they had *then* a
RIGHT to be afked,—fhould *afterwards* RE-
SIST *that very* law, which they had *then*

R   N O

NO RIGHT to difobey,—the conftitution, *muft lodge*, fome UNCONTROULABLE POWER SOMEWHERE, or, the government in fuch a cafe, would be INSTANTLY DISSOLVED.

Should fuch a bleffed form of government as *this*, which now only exifts in the *fublime* fpeculations of *modern politicians*, be once reduced to practice,—*then* indeed would be realized, that beautiful picture, feen by fome, in their mental eye, (" *whilft* " *in a fine phrenfy rolling*,") of the government, of ALL, by ALL. Oh glorious Æra! enviable ftate! which fome in their rapturous vifions fee, near at hand! For how much fuperior, both in happinefs, and duration, would it be even to that FIFTH MONARCHY,—which,—their forefathers likewife, in vifions, faw—*faft approaching*. But which, luckily for their defcendants,—who entertain the moft rooted averfion, to the *very name* of a MONARCHY,—is *not yet come*; and of which, to their great joy, they have *now no* expectation.

But however, 'till the commencement of that other illuftrious epoch, for which, the greateft and fageft politicians of this age, are fo devoutly wifhing; whatever may be the NUMBER of the people, whether FEW or MANY, who, not being by the CONSTITUTION, vefted in any participation of the POWER, of MAKING or EXECU-TING the laws,—fhall notwithftanding, take upon themfelves to DETERMINE,—WHAT LAWS they will OBEY, and WHAT, THEY WILL NOT, they certainly (whatever their phyfical power may be) *affume* a POWER in the ftate, to which they have NO RIGHT. Becaufe they both annihilate the government, and revert into a *ftate of nature*. For by fuch a conduct, they difclaim the RIGHT of the GOVERNOR or GOVERNORS to COMMAND, and if, HE or they, to whom the power of making and executing the laws in the ftate be intrufted, EXER-CISE his or their RIGHT, and DUTY, in the attempt to INFORCE them, meet with

RESISTANCE,

RESISTANCE,—the people who arrogated the power to themfelves, to which they had NO RIGHT, are certainly in the eye of truth and reafon the CRIMINALS, and not the LEGISLATORS and GOVERNORS,— as is the fafhionable opinion of the day, in oppofition even to common fenfe.

For, let us even fuppofe a cafe, in which, the people *think* the laws which they refufe to obey, to be very contrary to the *general* happinefs, of the fociety, for which the government was inftituted; and let them in reality be *ever fo much fo.* Now, though the legiflator can not be JUSTIFIED, in MAKING fuch a law, reference being made to the laws of *virtue, morality,* or *religion:* Yet when enacted, he has, from the very *nature, effence,* and *principles* of government, a RIGHT to INFORCE them. Neither can RESISTANCE in the fubjects, reference being had to the laws of *virtue* and *religion,* be JUSTIFIED.

Becaufe,

Becaufe, from the SAME NATURE of government, THEY. are BOUND to *obey* them.
Both parties indeed, would in fuch a cafe, be
guilty and AMENABLE to the LAWS of GOD;
wherever, I mean, thofe laws, have been made
known, both to the legiflator, and the people.
And as it is the reliance, which each party
has on it's own power, to fubdue the other,
which when UNRESTRAINED by RELIGION,
can ever induce either party to MAKE
AN APPEAL TO THE SWORD, when any
difference in opinion, occurs between the
governor and the governed,—NOTHING,
can more EFFECTUALLY EVINCE the IM-
PORTANCE and NECESSITY of RELIGION,
to the SUPPORT of CIVIL GOVERNMENT.
It's aid being we fee, INDISPENSABLY
REQUISITE for the INSTRUCTION, BOTH
of the governors, and the governed, in
THEIR DUTY; and for the fupply of both
with HIGHER PRINCIPLES, and more FOR-
CIBLE MOTIVES, to fubdue their paffions,
and to regulate their refpective conduct to
each other; by SUBJUGATING the DE-

SIRES OF BOTH PARTIES, to the WILL of GOD. REVERENCE, therefore for the DEITY and OBEDIENCE to HIS REVEALED LAWS, and a SACRED ATTENTION to ALL the MEANS, which LEAD to such an END, are both the great CEMENT in EVERY PART, and the GRAND KEY-STONE in the WHOLE FRAME of CIVIL GOVERNMENT. Because, it is evident, that without the controul of religion, there is no power to curb the DESPOTIC WILL of the GOVERNOR, but, the *fear* of the *rebellion* of the *subjects;* and also, that, WITHOUT IT'S INFLUENCE, NO RESTRAINT remains upon the STILL MORE LICENTIOUS WILLS OF THE SUBJECTS, when, all dread is removed from them, of the *ability* of the *ruler,* to *controul.* In either case,

> is plucked from curb'd licence,
> The muzzle of restraint, and the wild dog
> Shall flesh his tooth on every innocent...

This

This CONCLUSION, you perceive, Sir, not only flows directly and uninterruptedly from the foregoing PREMISES; but likewife as you will find, *neceffarily* gives rife to OTHER STREAMS OF KNOWLEDGE, with the SOURCES of which, you feem at prefent to be unacquainted; as they are certainly not to be difcovered, by any directions, which have been pointed out by *Mr. Locke.* But, as thefe more properly belong to ANOTHER PART OF OUR ENQUIRY, and WILL, in THAT, be evidently difcernible; I fhall now feize this opportunity, of leaving you for a time to your lucubrations, that you may, if you choofe *fo* to employ the interval, MEDITATE upon this MOST VALUABLE, and confequently moft IMPORTANT of ALL SUBJECTS, which can either folicit man's attention, or engage his enquiry.

I am, Sir,

Yours, &c.

LETTER

———

LETTER VII.

SIR,

AS, from the little knowledge I have of human nature, I apprehend, it to be moft probable, that you have rather been endeavouring to find fome broken link in the chain, by which my foregoing premifes and conclufions are united, than to difcover, what other links will naturally append to it, I fhall in this letter, adapt myfelf precifely to fuch a meditation. For though I have not the fmalleft apprehenfion of your difcovery, of a *flaw* in that *concatenation*, yet I doubt not, but you

imagine,

imagine, that you have an inftrument within your reach, by which you fhall be able
to fhatter, the *whole chain,* into a thoufand fragments.

For, I apprehend, that you are ready
to oppofe to thefe principles, and conclufions, *that* fophifm, if I may be allowed
the expreffion, " *millies decies repetitum* "
with little variation in *form,*—viz.—" that,
" as the *very end,* for which government
" was inftituted, was the *general* happinefs
" of the fociety, it is *therefore abfurd* to
" fuppofe, that the MAJORITY *can* be *bound*
" to OBEY thofe commands, laws, and in-
" ftitutions, to which, they have not by fome
" means or other, given their affent, which
" is the UNALIENABLE RIGHT of ALL
" MANKIND."

But, Sir, be pleafed to confider, that it
is upon the *truth* of the TWO following

S

POSITIONS, that ALL GOVERNMENT WHAT-
SOEVER was ORIGINALLY founded.

Firſt, that the MULTITUDE, are NOT
the BEST JUDGES, of what, *will moſt* conduce even to their *own individual,* much
leſs therefore, to the *general* happineſs of
a ſociety.

And *ſecondly,* that, if, they COULD diſ-
cover the MEANS, to this GREAT END;—
they would not VOLUNTARILY impoſe
upon themſelves, thoſe *reſtraints* which *are*
neceſſary for it's attainment.

The truth of the FIRST of theſe poſitions, is *evident* from hence,—that the *bulk*
of the people, can neither ſpare a ſufficient portion of time, to allot to *reflection,*
nor conſequently therefore have the requiſite opportunity, for the acquiſition of that
portion of *reaſon, underſtanding,* and *wiſdom,*
which is abſolutely neceſſary, for the *ſe-*
lection,

lection, of the *properest* MEANS to that END, out of a *great variety* of circumſtances,—whoſe GENERIC, and SPECIFIC DIFFERENCES, can *not* be aſcertained, without much cloſeneſs of attention, and exactneſs of diſcrimination. For ſurely, LEGISLATION conſidered as a SCIENCE, at leaſt requires *as good* ABILITIES for it's ACQUISITION as *any other* SCIENCE; and when conſidered as an ART, demands as *habitual* an application, and *ſkill* for it's PRACTICE, as *any other* ART.

The truth of the *ſecond* propoſition, is *not leſs* evident than that of the firſt. For, were the *multitude,* capable of *diſtinguiſhing,* what *is moſt* conducive to THEIR GENERAL GOOD; upon WHAT PRINCIPLE, I befeech you, could they be INDUCED to CHOOSE it, in *preference,* to the *immediate* gratification of ſome *deſire, inclination,* and *paſſion, eſpecially* when,—as in the caſe ſuppoſed,—there was *no expectation* of *any*

S 2   puniſhment,

punifhment, or controul whatfoever, to *in-force* it? Will you fay,—they might de-rive fufficient motives from the LAWS OF VIRTUE, or of MORALITY. But, before you can maintain this,—you muft have totally forgotten, what, has been already *fully* pro-ved,—that *had* fuch a pofition as this, been *originally* admitted, as the JUST *principle* of ALL government, viz:—that the *people,* OUGHT either to *make,* or, *when made,* give *their approbation* to the LAWS, before they fhould be obliged to OBEY them; then,— NO SUCH LAWS as THOSE of VIRTUE, COULD EVER have been DISCOVERED by human reafon, for the regulation of hu-man conduct. For, it has been clearly fhown, that THEY, are all built, upon the EXPERIENCE, which is derived from the UTILITY of GOVERNMENT, in COMPEL-LING the multitude, to SACRIFICE the gra-tification of their PRIVATE, inclinations, and SELFISH paffions, to the GENERAL happinefs of the SOCIETY; and, that from

thence,

thence, thefe GENERAL LAWS of VIRTUE and MORALITY, were DEDUCED; to com-.prehend, within the bonds of their obli-.gation, ALL MANKIND.

If however, you will *reject this fyftem of mine*, as too novel for your appetite, and will go back to the old fyftem of *any other* writer, upon the ORIGIN of MORAL OBLIGATION; you will find;—that your argument, by " *proving too much,—proves no-* " *thing.*" For, if the laws of *virtue* and *morality, are able* to INDUCE the multitude to *facrifice* upon *all* occafions, their own PRIVATE GRATIFICATIONS to the PUBLIC GOOD,—then it follows,—that *all civil government,* is altogether unnecefTary, and ufelefs, either to the guidance, or reftraint of men's volitions, and inclinations. Whereas to produce this GREAT END, was *really* the SOLE PURPOSE of IT'S FIRST INSTITUTION.

Will

Will you then maintain, that however *falſe*, *ſuch* a poſition, WOULD have been *formerly;* yet as GOD has been pleaſed to REVEAL HIS WILL, to ALL mankind, there can be no objection to the admiſſion of SUCH a PRINCIPLE of government *now;* becauſe, CHRISTIANITY, ſupplies ALL MEN, with a SUFFICIENT MOTIVE to SUCH a conduct?

If *this*, ſhould be your argument; permit me to remind you; *firſt*, that, as chriſtianity ſupplies motives, *equally efficacious* to the *governors*, as to the *governed;* by *parity* of *reaſoning*, there is much *leſs neceſſity* NOW, to admit the people into any *participation* of the *legiſlative power*,— than there was *formerly;* becauſe there is *now* therefore by your own confeſſion, an *additional reſtraint* upon the TYRANNY of GOVERNORS. And CHRISTIANITY, certainly *does not* ſupply the people, with *that knowledge*, which is *neceſſary* for making

CHANGES

CHANGES in governments; though, *it* furnifhes them, with *that wifdom*, which is *requifite*, for THEIR OBEDIENCE to governors. For it even gives us, *particular*
caution, " to BEWARE of THOSE,—who
" are GIVEN to CHANGE."

Secondly, had you been aware of the
confequences, which *follow* from *this* argument,—they would have made you :" *ftart*
" *afide, like a broken bow.*" For fuch an
argument, by the fubftitution of *another*
principle, inftantly *deprives* the people of
their claim, to a *fhare* in the *legiflation;*—
upon the *pene divinum* plea,—of NATU-
RAL RIGHT.

Thirdly, if, becaufe, *God* has vouchfafed
to *inftruct* man in his duty, we are *therefore* according to *your fyftem* of *logic*, to
conclude, that ALL MEN WILL NECESSA-
RILY UNDERSTAND, and PRACTISE it;
this happens unfortunately to you, to be

a

a conclusion, which *daily experience* contradicts, from the *very evidence* of your own, and your friends conduct: For, though the christian religion inculcates. into it's votaries, universal SUBMISSION to *rulers*, there is not a day passes over our heads, in which, either *you*, or *some* of *your* associates, do not contradict this, by inculcating, NOT OBEDIENCE, but RESISTANCE to government, as the GRAND DUTY; of SUBJECTS.

But, if this conclusion were not even *thus irreconcileable* with FACT;—yet, *mark well*, I beseech you,—what still *must* be, the *melancholy tendency* of it's *consequences.* For though, certainly such a conclusion; might be *productive* of the *most* IMPORTANT benefits, by raising a storm, which would EXTIRPATE every *root*, and *branch*, of our RELIGIOUS ESTABLISHMENT; "a " *consummation; by you,* (no doubt,) *devout-* " *ly to be wished;*" yet unluckily,—it would

in

in it's fury,—hurry away with it likewife,
—every timber, brick, and ftone of every
diffenting minifter's meeting-houfe in the
whole world.

For, admitting this doctrine to be true;
it would then be an act of *robbery*, in
every minifter of *every* denomination, to demand *contributions*, any more, than *tithes*
from their congregations. Or at leaft, it
would be but a *fwindling trick*, in them,
to cozen their congregations out of their
money, by pretending,—to *fell* them a *com-
modity*, of which they were in full poffeffion, without the payment for it, even of
a fingle doit.

I have fome confolation however, in
thinking, that how frequently foever, fuch
a doctrine as this, I am now combating,
may be advanced;—that it arifes only from
the *laudable motive*, of *rendering* our PRE-
SENT CIVIL and RELIGIOUS ESTABLISH-

T

MENT

MENT CONTEMPTIBLE, in the eyes of
IT'S SUBJECTS; and by thefe means, *en-*
couraging them, as far as can be done,
with fafety, to *overturn* it, and bury it's
doctrines, and it's minifters, in the ruins.

For, I cannot think, that *even* YOU,
SIR, and then it is impoffible to conceive,
that ANY ONE ELSE, would be willing to
put *fuch* a doctrine, to the only *fure teft*
of it's truth,—EXPERIENCE. That is to
fay,—to try,—whether the multitude,—(I
mean,)—not only barely the *majority*, but
an almoft infinite number *above* a majority, (for if a majority has a RIGHT, a
fortiori, a *larger* number has ftill *more*
right, to MAKE LAWS) are not BEST
QUALIFIED, to ENACT LAWS for the *ge-*
neral happinefs; and whether, they will
not MOST READILY OBEY them, when, *all*
temporal penalties are removed; and nothing remains to inforce them, but merely
the more *remote influence of religious fanc-*
tions.

tions. For it should seem, that the *National Assembly* of *France*, even in *their* MUL-TIPLICITY OF EXPERIMENTS, all founded, upon the REVERSE of every conclusion, deduced from *experience* of the *nature* of *man*, have not *yet* advanced *quite so far*, as to try *this*; as they have neither given at present, a MAJORITY of the PEOPLE, a RIGHT of MAKING LAWS, nor even of CHOOSING REPRESENTATIVES. Yet THEY have in *reserve*, a *much more powerful engine* of their own contrivance, to ENFORCE OBEDIENCE, than as *they* think, ANY REVELATION FROM GOD, can possibly be;—you already guess that I mean, —their intended *frame* of *institutes*,—for the EDUCATION of a CITIZEN.

'Till therefore, the legislators of *other* nations are become *even wiser*, than those *enlightened ones* in France, who have discovered REVEALED RELIGION to be a JEST,—and INJUSTICE to be NO VICE;—

and

and that PILLAGE, ROBBERY, MURDER, and SACRILEGE, are the FOUR CARDI-NAL VIRTUES; the fubjects of *other* nations, muft be *content* to OBEY the *laws*, of their refpective governments, though they fhould not happen to *enact* them. Nay; though they fhould, even chance to think, that a law does *not* contribute to the *greateft general* happinefs;—they are ftill bound to obedience,—from a. PRINCIPLE; which is the *foundation* of ALL GOVERN-MENT, and therefore paramount to all other confiderations. For where ever, a *legifla-ture* exifts, though it be compofed of *fal-lible* men, it follows, from the very *defini-tion* of the term, that *it* has a *right* to MAKE, and the *executive power*, has a RIGHT to enforce *fuch laws*, as feem to THEM, *beft* calculated to produce the *general* happinefs: and *fubmiffion* to them, is the DU-TY of ALL the SUBJECTS. THIS is a PRINCIPLE of UNIVERSAL OBLIGATION, which is common to ALL LAWS, from the

VERY ESSENCE of the *thing*, whether, they
are laws made by the legiflature of a *particular* ftate,—whether, they are the LAWS
of *virtue*, or of *morality*, deduced by men's
reafoning faculties, or *fanEtioned* by the
REVELATION, of an INFALLIBLE LEGIS-
LATOR.

. *Strange*, and *almoft inconceivable*, as the
foregoing pofition may appear, to many at
firft fight; yet, it is in *faEt*, not only
perfeEtly intelligible, but likewife *very eafily
proved*. For, were *individuals* left to themfelves to determine, when even *thofe general laws*, of *morality* and *religion*, fhould
be obeyed, and when not; *many*,—or *all*,
—*even* perhaps of THEM, would NOT AP-
PEAR to be *always* conducive to the *general good*. On the contrary, it would appear to the fallible optics of the wifeft
men, that GREATER GOOD in *particular*
cafes, might arife from the non-obfervance,
than from aEting in *conformity* to them.

But

But why then, it may be afked, did *men* deduce *fuch general* laws, and reduce them into a fyftem of morality, and why is UNIVERSAL OBEDIENCE to them required? For how then, can fuch a requifition, be for the *general good?*

The anfwer, is, plain, and obvious and even familiar. Becaufe, though *more apparent* good, might even arife, from a NON-COMPLIANCE with them, in fome *particular* cafes; yet, were a *permiffion* given to each *individual,* to *judge* for *himfelf,* *when,* obedience to them, was *proper,* and *when not; fuch* a permiffion, would be in *effect,* an ABROGATION of them AS LAWS, and would often authorize the perpetration of murder, adultery, robbery, and every fpecies of injuftice, for the *prevention* of which, they were, in ALL CASES intended.

Precifely

Precisely therefore, for the same reason also, it is, that *such* a permission can *not* be granted to *subjects;* which, is not only contended for as a *theoretical truth*, but DEMANDED as the NATURAL UNALIENABLE RIGHT of MAN, and of the PRACTICE of which, *through all it's consequences,* it is affirmed to be an *act* of *injustice, cruelty, oppression,* and *tyranny* in *any government,* to deprive *any,* even the lowest, of it's members. For if it were, the LAWS of the STATE, would likewise, in this case, as the *laws* of *virtue* in the former, *be in effect* ANNULLED,—government would be dissolved;—men would again fall into that very *state* of *nature,* and of ANARCHY, which involves them in infinitely more misery, than, the very WORST FORM of CIVIL GOVERNMENT, can POSSIBLY PRODUCE.

Hence then it follows, that if an human legislature, even *enjoins* it's subjects,
                                                either

either to *omit* any action, of which, by
the *laws* of *virtue*, or *religion*, the *omiſſion*
appears to them, to be wrong; or *com-
mands* them to *perform* ſome action, which
when brought to the ſame TEST, *appears*
to *them* to be VICIOUS or WICKED; it
does not then become their DUTY to *reſiſt* and *rebel*, but they are bound QUIET-
LY to *ſubmit* to the *loſs* of the ſeeming
good, however great it might be, which
they would have obtained, by a *compliance*
with the laws; or to any *other* inconvenience or *pain*, which they might ſuſtain,
in conſequence of *diſobedience*. Exactly, as
in all other caſes whatſoever, where we
would regulate our conduct, by the rules
of *virtue* or *morality*, whenever any pleaſure, or ſeeming advantage, might be obtained by the *gratification* of the PASSI-
ONS, *ſuch* pleaſure and advantage, *muſt* be
ſacrificed, to the *laws* of *virtue*, and *religion*.

However *wrong* therefore, a legiſlature
may be in *enacting ſome* laws, yet, the
people

people are ftill bound to *obey* them, unlefs
fuch laws are deftructive of fome particular *conftitution*, by making a *breach* in the
compact, *between* the GOVERNED and the
GOVERNORS; in that PARTICULAR FORM
of government; and for *which breach*, that
VERY CONSTITUTION has PROVIDED a
REMEDY, by AUTHORISING in *fuch cafes*,
the PEOPLE'S DISBOEDIENCE. But a *refufal* of *obedience* in the *fubjects*, to the
ACTS of the LEGISLATURE, much more
refiftance or rebellion, muft be in ALL
OTHER CASES, at ALL TIMES, offences of
the moft complicated guilt, and crimes of
the deepeft dye. For, the *magnitude* of the
guilt, muft not only be eftimated,—by the
uncontroulable violence of the PASSIONS, in
the firft, and more immediate agents;—but
alfo, by the *number*, and heinoufnefs of
the crimes, of which, *they* are only *medi-
ately*, or even *remotely* the *caufes*;—and
likewife by the unmeafurable inundation
of evils,—which, iffuing forth from both

U   thefe

these fources,—raging in a refiftlefs torrent,
—muft neceffarily overwhelm the *whole
kingdom*,—in ruin, and defolation.

·So truly *trifling, falfe* and *fophiftical,*
(and. I. fhould add contemptible, but for
fear of giving you offence) are thefe AR-
GUMENTS, and ALL OTHERS likewife, which,
are founded upon the fandy, or rather
undifcoverable foundation, of the NATU-
RAL RIGHTS OF MEN. Notwithftanding
therefore, the NATIONAL ASSEMBLY OF
FRANCE, have advanced THEM. as the
FIRST PRINCIPLES OF ALL GOVERNMENT,
in their DECLARATION OF RIGHTS,

> Which, now to fenfe, and now to nonfenfe, leaning,
> Mean not, but blunder round about, a meaning.

and though, even the PEOPLE have SANC-
TIONED *celles lanternes,* by the penalty of
the *lantern poft;* yet, the venerable MINO-
RITY of that motley body, enlifted under
the

the banners of REASON, muſt ever brand them with reprobation, and rejeſt them with contempt.

To our moſt ſincere wiſhes, and hopes, therefore, may we not add alſo, our firm truſt, and confidence, that theſe " *unſubſtan-* " *tial pageants,*" called NATURAL RIGHTS, are now " *diſſolved,*" and will be no longer

> —— *blown with reſtleſs violence* *round about the pendant world.*

That *you,* may have time, by conſidering what has been already ſaid, to form the ſame hope, breathe the ſame wiſh, and at-tain to the ſame truſt and confidence,—I ſhall conclude this letter, remaining

Sir,

Yours, &c.

U 2　　　　　　LETTER

LETTER VIII.

SIR,

I HOPE you have had now sufficient leisure, most *maturely* to weigh, the *words*, NATURAL RIGHTS, and to exile them for ever from your mind, to the regions of nonsense; where only they could have their birth, from the union of ERROR, with ANARCHY. For, if those, which are called RIGHTS were NATURAL; —then GOVERNMENT would be UNNATURAL. And if all men claim it, as their NATURAL RIGHT to DO AS THEY PLEASE, NO GOVERNMENT CAN POSSIBLY EXIST.

The

The only queſtion therefore, which a
ſubjeƈt can aſk himſelf, under ANY SPECIES
OF GOVERNMENT, is *not,* what RIGHTS
ſhould, I WISH to have, and therefore may
claim as INDEFEASIBLE;—but,—

First, WHAT ARE the RIGHTS,—to which,
—I am *entitled,* by the CONSTITUTION of
the government, under which, I live.

Secondly, whether, ſuch others, as I ſhould
wiſh to have,—WOULD be COMPATIBLE
with the preſent *particular* RIGHTS, and
general wiſhes and *welfare* of my fellow
ſubjeƈts.

Thirdly, whether I, and thoſe who entertain the ſame inclinations, and opinions with myſelf,—are *likely* to obtain them
from the legiſlature, without DISTURBING,
—the TRANQUILITY,—PEACE,—and HAP-
PINESS,—of the ſociety?

For,

For, the GENERAL HAPPINESS of the WHOLE kingdom, is certainly the GRAND END, to which, every *law* should tend; even *more invariably*, than the needle, when touched by the loadstone, does actually turn towards the pole. Where, therefore, under any constitution of government, the legislature enacts any law, which can *impart* a GOOD, to *some*, which they did *not before* enjoy, or *remove* from them, some INCONVENIENCE, which they before sustained,—*without* SUBJECTING the rest, to INJURY or INCONVENIENCE:—*there*,—the government is IMPROVED.

In such a case, however, the legislature, should most cautiously attend, to the *very wide* distance, there is, between the REMOVAL of an *actual pain*, or positive inconvenience; and the CONFERRING of NEW POWER.

For,

For, to the *former*, a man may be said to have *some claim*, from the laws of morality, and religion. *To* the *other*, he can not pretend, to set up even any *moral* plea whatsoever; but there may be not only many political, and constitutional, but likewise even some *moral* objections *against* it. So likewise, even in the *removal only* of pain, or some positive inconvenience, the legislature, should not only attend to the *immediate*, but also, to the remoter consequences, which may result from it; as to the probable conversion of the *freedom* from PAST RESTRAINT, into the *acquisition* of FUTURE POWER.

For no argument, can possibly be more absurd, or contradictory, in *any set of men*, even, *supposing* the *fact* to be *true*, upon which they build it? than to pretend,—that they have a *claim* to any such indulgent relaxation, of the rigour of the laws, —*because, whilst* they were *under this re-straint,*

ſtraint,—they were *quiet* and *peaceable* ſubjeĉts. As *this,* only proves, that the laws
had anſwered the purpoſe, for which they
were enaĉted; viz. that of making quiet
ſubjeĉts of thoſe,—who were reſtleſs and
refraĉtory, before the paſſing of thoſe laws.
But, BECAUSE, it was for the *very purpoſe*
of *producing* this *effeĉt,* that the *reſtraint
was* layed upon them;—FOR THAT VERY
reaſon,—their *paſt loyalty* and *obedience,* under *ſuch* circumſtances, however great they
might have been,—*can not* poſſibly, be *any*
PLEDGE, or SECURITY for their *future
conduĉt,—when,—that* VERY RESTRAINT,—
ſhould be REMOVED.

A more ample, and indiſputable illuſtra-
tion, and confirmation, of the *truth* of
theſe obſervations, can *not* be given,—than
that,—with which, you yourſelf have been
ſo kind as to ſupply us, in your twelfth
letter, page 122.

For

For there you fay, " time was when
" (the Church of England) pretended, to
" *fear where no fear was,* and being then
" VIGOROUS,—her cries were heard, *as the*
" *roaring of a lion.* Of late, fhe has
" BEEN SO FEEBLE, that, WE ONLY
" AMUSE OURSELVES WITH THEM, and
" *now* the DANGER is *really* TRANSFER-
" RED FROM US, TO THEMSELVES."

Now, what does, this very *plain,* and
explicit declaration, amount to,—BUT THIS
very kind information,—that we were FOOLS,
to *take away* the *penal laws,* againft you,
and your friends; for, that YOU, having
now acquired power,—notwithftanding all
your *pretences* to liberality of fentiment,
and chriftian charity;—to loyalty to the
King, and love to your Country;—notwithftanding your claim to a *monopoly* of *all* the
wifdom and *virtue* in the kingdom,—WILL
eagerly feize *every opportunity,* (and you
go on, to point out the opportunities, which

X   will

will be afforded) of USING that VERY
POWER,—to the DESTRUCTION of your
truly *liberal*, and *generous* benefactors.

Permit me however, from REAL TEN-
DERNESS, to you, and your friends;—do
not start,—you may venture to believe it
without hesitation, for my conduct has been
always firm and manly towards them; (the
open opposer of their opinions and doctrines,—but more than once a cordial friend,
and warm advocate for the men who held
them,) to recommend to you, *more caution*,
not only in your declarations of your *future intentions*,—but likewise,—in your *present constant exhibitions*, of your rooted prejudices;—your bigotted animosity,—and your
unchristian hatred,—to the *Church of England*,—it's *doctrines*,—and it's *ministers*. *Per-
secuting* the latter as you do,—which is, *as
far as you can*,—in their literary fame,—
wherever, you can get the command of a
periodical publication,—however *liberal they
may*

may be in their fentiments, towards *all* other feêts. Mifreprefenting likewife, thofe who affociate with you, from principles of liberality, and of chriftian charity,—as court- ing your company, for the fake of inftruc- tion,—and as leaving the fociety, of their bigotted brethren of the eftablifhment,— from their predileêtion, for the *more en- larged fentiments* of *your* feêt.

'Remember, Sir, that the LION of the foreft, alfo, does not *always roar,*—but may fometimes condefcend to fuffer, fome of the lower tribes of animals, (even per- haps fome of that fpecies, which moft re- femble, and moft delight in imitating men,) to play around him,—admit them into fome familiarity,—proteêt them from their moft ferocious enemies,—and divert himfelf with their gambols,—though they fhould be ex- preffive only of their vanity, and their weaknefs. But if, from this indulgence, they, growing bold, and petulant, fhould

miftake

miſtake his gentleneſs for ſupineneſs,—and his meekneſs for indifference,—and once more rouſing him from his repoſe,—he does but begin to ſhake his ſhaggy mane, and utter his deep-toned roar,—they would inſtantly be ſtruck aghaſt with horror,—and in a moment, ſcramble away to the firſt cover they could find, ſmall enough, to hide them, from his awakened fury, and tremendous ſtrength.

But, let us lay aſide metaphor, and re-turn to the ſubject, more immediately be-fore us. When, *again*, the executive and legiſlative powers, GIVE UP any power, with which by the conſtitution, they hap-pen to be entruſted,—and of which, they are conſcious,—the HAPPINESS of the so-CIETY, do not REQUIRE the EXERCISE; —becauſe the *exertion* of it, could only ſerve to the gratification of the paſſions, of thoſe, in whom thoſe powers are lodg-ed,—who have their *weakneſſes* and *frailties*

in

in *common* with all other men :—in *that*
cafe *likewife*,—there is,—we fay,—an alteration in the government, and a *reformation* in the *conftitution*. The UTMOST CARE,
and CAUTION however, muſt *alſo* be uſed
on SUCH AN OCCASION, in every conſtitution, where, the *legiſlature*, *confiſts* of
DIFFERENT BRANCHES ;—to PREVENT the
POWER, which may thus be SURRENDER-
ED by ONE of them, from being TRANS-
FERRED to ANY, or ALL of the OTHERS.
For where this is the confequence,—the
balance of the conſtitution,—inſtead of being *amended*,—may be *totally deſtroyed*.

In any ſuch cafes likewife,—where,
the governors of the ſtate, do not of
their own accord, paſs ſuch laws,—the governed may under *all* the various forms,
of different conſtitutions,—perhaps, without
any breach, either of their *moral duty*, or
their *obedience* as *ſubjeſts*,—*petition* for alte-
rations ;—provided, they do ſo, with that
refpeſt,

respe&, which is *always due* from *subjects,*
to the *supreme power* in every state;—and
quietly SUBMIT, if, *that power.* think differently from them,—as to the PROPRIETY,
of *granting,* the objects of their petitions.
For, from it's decision, there can not poffibly be, under *any* government, ANY
LAWFUL APPEAL; nor even from it's ER-
RORS, and it's PREJUDICES, any RIGHT-
FUL REDRESS. ●

Very unacceptable, and even difagreeable
no doubt, must THESE TRUTHS appear to
thofe of our *modern political innovators,*—who
miftake every popular, propofed alteration,
for an excellent reformation, in a conftitution;—which is,—and long has been,
an object of admiration,—to fome states,
and of envy,—to others.—To thofe, who
deem an edifice to be increafing in beauty, the nearer it approaches, to a mere
exhibition of ruins.—To thofe, who fired by
their own enthufiafm, conceive every fugges-
tion

tion of fancy, to be an object of experience.—To those, who more lukewarm in
themselves, but heated, by mixing in frequent crouds, receive from, and communi-
cate, the flame of their prejudices, and
their paffions, to each other.—To those,
who however really ignorant they are,
yet by a conftant reciprocation of flattery,
believe themfelves to be irradiated with
fupereminent light, and to be poffeffed of
the utmoft ftore of knowledge.—To thofe,
who not being often admitted under vault-
ed roofs, miftake the reverberations of
their own voices within, for fhouts of
approbation, from crouds, without.—To thofe,
who,—becaufe hundreds of men, of genuine genius and learning, who live retired
in their rural fhades, content themfelves
only with defpifing their *book-making*, and
their *puffing*, (but not chufing to encounter their virulence and abufe, do not
reply to them) prefume therefore, from
the filence of thofe, who differ from them,
that

that their own opinions, are deemed, to
be, incapable of refutation.—To thofe,
who valuing themfelves upon their art,—
cunning,—and addrefs, though they have
not much knowledge of the world, and
ftill lefs of human nature, fancy, that the
real roughnefs, rudenefs, and fiercenefs of
their difpofitions, are not perceived, on
account of the fometimes affected fmooth-
nefs, foftnefs, and fubtlenefs of their outward demeanor;—and imagine that where
a fmile is forced, upon the rigid, unre-
laxing mufcles of their mouths,—there can
be no fufpicion, of rancour, rankling in
the heart.

In all thefe,—and fuch as thefe charac-
ters, however various may be their divifions and fubdivifions,—however fimilar they
may be in fome features,—and diffimilar
in others,—yet in ALL of them,—no doubt,
—THESE TRUTHS will almoft equally excite difpleafure, and perhaps exactly in
proportion

proportion to the strength of the arguments in their support, exasperate their
resentment.

Yet, though I am unwilling, to be the
cause of ·pain to any one, and if I know
my own heart, never intend to excite it,
except, when, as I am now bound in duty, for the promotion of the happiness of
others:—of so great importance, do I deem
these truths to be;—that short as this letter is, I shall here conclude it; that you,
and my other readers may have the more
time, seriously to consider, and accurately
to weigh them;—and attentively to scru-
tinize into all the *numerous*,—and if neglected,—*dangerous, consequences*,—which follow
in their train.

For, however the almost sacred name of
LIBERTY, ·may be used as the denomination, of the darling object of the discon-
tented, under *any form* of government;

it

it is certainly very feldom fo employed, but, as a ftalking-horfe; whilft in reality, the LOVE of POWER, fkulking behind it, affords men an opportunity of aiming at the deftruction of every thing, which, whilft it exifts, obftructs their felfifh inclinations, or by it's extinction, fupplies them, with food for their PRIDE,—their AVARICE, —and their AMBITION.

" O for that warning voice, which he who faw
" Th' Apocalypfe, heard cry in heaven aloud."

But if *that*, be not any more permitted to reach the ear of mortals; let BRITONS however, be warned by a voice which now cries *aloud*, and *fpares not*, from the oppofite fhore. Which, bids the SONS of ALBION BEWARE, what experiments they try upon their conftitution, either in church or ftate;—bids them BEWARE,—of the FASCINATION from the *well founding words*,— PHILOSOPHY,—ENLIGHTENED TIMES,—LIBERTY,—and NATURAL RIGHTS;—left,—
inftead

inftead of finding the RETURN of a SA-
TURNIAN REIGN,—*they* fhould *fall* a *facri-
fice* to AMBITION,—PRIDE,—INJUSTICE,—
IGNORANCE,—and BARBARISM, marching
in the van;—or to,—FURY,—CRUELTY,—
DESPOTISM,—SLAUGHTER,—and DESOLA-
TION, maddening in the rear.

I am, Sir,

Yours, &c.

Y 2   LETTER

LETTER IX.

SIR,

HAVING now, not only, I truſt, totally DESTROYED every PLEA to the
CLAIM of any privileges in ſociety, from
the *natural* RIGHTS of men;—having alſo,
I doubt not, for ever *expelled* the *words*
from any future admiſſion, *amongſt* the
terms, which *appertain* to the SCIENCE of
POLITICS;—having likewiſe I hope, clearly, and evidently traced, the ORIGIN, and
PROGRESS of MORAL SCIENCE, through a
path, which though neglected by all former writers,—was the only one, in which
                                    they

they, *ought* to have proceeded;—and laftly,
—having pointed out the vaft care and
attention, with which, even *any* reformation ought to be made in ANY SPECIES
of GOVERNMENT;—it feems to me, to be
very probable, that in future,—for the
terms, NATURAL RIGHTS,—MORAL RIGHTS,
will in general be fubftituted. And perhaps, if NO CAUTION were given to prevent it; the LATTER words, might, at no
diftant time be ufed, as the FORMER have
long been;—only as *bugbears*, to frighten
every one, from *venturing* to *examine* the
TRUTH or FALSEHOOD of any propofition, fo entitled; upon the fuppofition, that
ALL POSITIONS which were SO CHARAC-
TERISED, *had a* CLAIM from EVERY ONE,
to an IMMEDIATE and UNHESITATING
ASSENT.

Thus perhaps, for inftance, it will now
be urged,—that as I do, and muft admit,
that the GENERAL HAPPINESS of the PEO-
PLE,

PLE, OUGHT to be the FUNDAMENTAL
PRINCIPLE of EVERY GOVERNMENT,—
and that as I alfo allow, that there are
DIFFERENT FORMS of government, SOME
of which, are furnifhed with BETTER
MEANS for that ONE GREAT END, than
others;—"therefore,—the MAJORITY, MUST
" at ALL TIMES, have a MORAL RIGHT
" to change, (for inftance) a conftitution,
" —which has intrufted an ARBITRARY
" POWER, in the hands of ONE MAN,—
" FOR ONE,—in which,—a power fo lia-
" ble to be abufed,—is CONTROULED,
" CHECKED, and REGULATED."

To prevent however, to the utmoft of
our power, ALL POSSIBLE ABUSE of the
terms, " MORAL RIGHTS," by ufing them,
without HAVING IDEAS ANNEXED TO
THEM,—it is neceffary to obferve; that
when they are applied to any *propofed*
ALTERATION, in the INTERNAL GOVERN-
MENT of a ftate, the expreffions,—MO-
RALLY

RALLY RIGHT,—and POLITICALLY RIGHT are, SYNONYMOUS.

For, THAT change can not be MORALLY right, which is POLITICALLY WRONG; nor politically RIGHT, which is MORALLY WRONG. The GENERAL HAPPINESS, BEING, the ONLY COMMON MEASURE of any one, and the fame change;—which, may be by fome men, denoted in thefe different manners.—The WORDS therefore are only different,—but the SENSE of both the expreffions, is the SAME.

For, fhould any one deny this, and fay, that it is very eafy to *conceive*, MANY CHANGES in governments, which though undoubtedly MORALLY RIGHT, would be POLITICALLY WRONG:—if, we do but advance one ftep further, and enquire, what is to be underftood, by this *pretended diftinction*: we fhall find it to turn out, to be nothing more,—than *this quibble;*—that

fome

some changes, may be conceived to be made in governments, which at CERTAIN TIMES, and under CERTAIN CIRCUMSTANCES, might be MORALLY RIGHT; which, at OTHER *certain times,* and under OTHER *certain circumstances,*—would be,—POLITICALLY WRONG. But then, *still* it will be found, that in THOSE SEASONS, and on THOSE OCCASIONS, WHEN they would be MORALLY, they *would* also, be POLITICALLY right; and on the contrary, and so always interchangeably, that at THOSE SEASONS, and upon THOSE OCCASIONS, that they *would* be POLITICALLY,—they *would* also be, MORALLY WRONG.

But in answer to the particular position just stated; it must be observed, that considering it, in the light, either of an UNIVERSAL or GENERAL PROPOSITION, no one can possibly be MORE FALSE; as evidently follows, from EVERY PROOF, which has been ALREADY ESTABLISHED.

But,

But, that *there* MAY *be* CASES SUP-
POSED, in which, the people might law-
fully change an arbitrary form of government, into a more limitted one, BECAUSE,
there MAY BE CASES, where, fuch an act,
would be no infringement of any man's
RIGHT, nor occafion an *injury* to *any man*,
—I am ready to grant.

Thus for inftance, let us fuppofe a cafe,
in which, a *tyrant*, by *death*, or *fome other
caufe* of INCAPACITY, not only lets fall,
but can never be able again, to refume
the reins of government; and that the conftitution has not eftablifhed any fettled rule
of fucceffion. Here, the appointment of a
fucceffor, being left dependent upon the
choice of the people,—no doubt, the pofition is *fo far true*, that in fuch a cafe,
the *electors may*,—becaufe, *no right* is in-
fringed,—*change* the conftitution.

Z   For,

For, the *government* is *then* for a *moment diſſolved;* and the multitude are returned to their *original ſtate of nature.* If then, they deſire again to live in a ſtate of CIVIL SOCIETY, and GOVERNMENT, which they *will* wiſh to do, if they have retained their ſenſes:—they certainly *may* either appoint another governor, with the *ſame* powers, as were intruſted to the *former,* only making choice of *one,* whom they deem to be a *wiſer,* and a *better* man;—or, by appointing *others,* either to ſome *participation* in his power, or indeed, by dividing the *whole* of it, either amongſt *ſome few,* or a GREAT MANY in number, hope, and endeavour to eſcape the evils which aroſe, as they think, from placing the *deſpotic* or *arbitrary power,* which MUST ALWAYS EXIST SOMEWHERE,—in the hands of ONLY ONE MAN.

In ſuch a caſe, no doubt the people do not do wrong, and may do right in
attempting

attempting to *new-model* the government; becaufe, they *are* then, *precifely* in the fame fituation, except having had the advantage of experience, in which, they were, —when they, *at firft* agreed to inftitute a government. Though it muft be obferved, that even in this inftance, the *innoxioufnefs* of fuch an attempt, is altogether limitted to thofe cafes, where the new form can be modelled, without ANARCHY, and CONFUSION; and the CONSEQUENT CRIMES, which are attendant upon fuch a ftate. The PREVENTION of which, is the GRAND BLESSING of EVERY FORM of GOVERNMENT, and RENDERS the WORST, INFINITELY PREFERABLE, to NONE.

But in any OTHER cafe,—that is to fay, —whilft the government *actually exifts*,— they can not for the reafons, which I have affigned above, have any RIGHT,— but MUST DO WRONG, to DISSOLVE the government,—and revert to a ftate of na-

Z 2   ture,

ture, upon EVERY PRINCIPLE WHATSO-
EVER,—upon which,—either GOVERNMENT,
or the LAWS of VIRTUE or MORALITY,
CAN POSSIBLY BE FOUNDED. For, a ma-
jority, has NO MORE RIGHT, to TRANS-
GRESS ANY of THOSE LAWS, nor confe-
quently " TO DO EVIL THAT GOOD MAY
" COME OF IT," than, *any* SINGLE INDI-
VIDUAL: But, in a ftate of REBELLION,
or of WAR,—it is CERTAIN that " EVIL
" MUST be DONE,"—though it be quite
UNCERTAIN, whether,—" ANY GOOD will
" COME OF IT."

The *firft method*, which I have affigned,
in the foregoing cafe, which I have fuppofed,—from which,—the people may hope
to have a *better* government, arife out of
the afhes of the former;—was moft probably, the *firft experiment*, which was tried.
They refolved to ufe, and probably did
exercife the utmoft care, caution, and cir-
cumfpeƈtion, as they thought, in the fe-
leƈtion

lection and choice of a *new* governor. But, fuch were the evils, which attended even *fuch* a *temporary*, though fcarcely more than a *momentary* RELAPSE into a STATE of NATURE, and of ANARCHY, that repeated trials foon taught them,— that it was MUCH WORSE for mankind, to INCUR the CERTAIN EVIL, than even, to rifk a *chance*, after the UNCERTAIN GOOD.

From further reflection and experience, they were no long time in learning,—that neither the MANY, nor EVEN the FEW, had WISDOM or VIRTUE enough, to raife the HIGHEST WISDOM, and the GREATEST VIRTUE, to the most exalted rank, and moft extenfive power.

From hence then, they concluded,—as they were well warranted by their know-ledge of facts, and perfectly authorifed by the conclufions of their reafon, that an HEREDITARY SUCCESSION, was not only

beft

beſt calculated for the avoidance of the miſeries, they had ſuſtained by ſo tumultous an election, but likewiſe, for the acquiſition of that good, at which they had aimed, by their ſolicitude in the CHOICE.

In *ſome* other caſes perhaps, though certainly in *much fewer*, men have ſeized the opportunity, which, the *diſſolution* of the government gave them, to adopt, *one*, or *other*, of the *other* METHODS I have mentioned; though EXPERIENCE, has CERTAINLY SHOWN, that it has, VERY SELDOM been attended with *much melioration*, of their *condition*. For, the ABSOLUTE POWER STILL EXISTS, though it be ever ſo much divided, and ſubdivided; and though therefore in theſe caſes, there muſt indeed be an UNION OF WILLS, before it can bring OPPRESSION upon the PEOPLE, —yet, it frequently happens, (as there are always *motives* exiſting to *form* ſuch an union) that when formed, it wields an

iron

iron rod of oppreffion, fo extenfive in length, and fo deftructive by it's weight; —that the hand of ONE *man*, could not even raife, much lefs, direct it.

But in moft cafes, where, a CONSTITU-TION has been formed, which AMPLY provides CHECKS, and CONTROULS, upon both the LEGISLATIVE, and EXECUTIVE POWERS of the government, for the pro-duction of the *greateft poffible general hap-pinefs;*—it has rather been the effect, of what we *foolifhly* call ACCIDENT, than of any SETTLED DESIGN, or REGULAR ADAP-TATION of MEANS to ENDS.* Partly occa-fioned by the ebullitions of men's paffions, which at the time, no reafon could jufti-fy, though even from them, good was af-terwards educed; and when therefore, the firft agents were criminal, though their actions,

* See my *Sermon* on the KING's RECOVERY.

actions were beneficial. And partly, by events, of which no human fagacity could forefee even their birth, and certainly much lefs, their confequences.

· To SUCH CAUSES, under the direction of heaven, do we, for the moſt part owe, OUR OWN MOST EXCELLENT CON-STITUTION, the parts of which, are upon the WHOLE, fo nicely balanced, and regularly adjuſted; that, the COMMUNITY has nothing to fear; from any UNCONTROUL-ED TYRANNY of the EXECUTIVE POWER, though it is HEREDITARY, under CER-TAIN RESTRICTIONS; nothing to dread,—from any unavoidable IGNORANCE, or rather CAPRICE, in the legiſlature;—nor any thing to tremble at, from the UNRULY PASSIONS, and LICENTIOUS WILLS of the PEOPLE. The *lower ranks* of *fociety*, owe *their fecurity*, to the *fhare* intruſted to *numbers* of *them*, in the CHOICE of ONE of the CONSTITUENT PORTIONS of the

LEGISLATURE;

LEGISLATURE; and the WHOLE SOCIETY
is indebted for IT'S PRESERVATION, to
the EXCLUSION of the MULTITUDE, from
the POWER of MAKING LAWS, in themfelves; and the INTRUSTING SUFFICI-
ENT FORCE in the EXECUTIVE POWER,
to COMPEL THEM to OBEY thofe, which
are made by the perfons, in whom, that
power is vefted;—whether, according to
the people's OWN CONCEPTIONS of them,
they HAPPEN, either to be APPROVED, or
DISAPPROVED.

The more effectually however, to fecure
an attention in the legiflature, to THE
PEOPLE'S RIGHTS,—their INTEREST,—and
their HAPPINESS;—they at ftated intervals,
have an OPPORTUNITY of REMOVING
THOSE REPRESENTATIVES from their
TRUST, who have given affent to laws,
which, after the CONSTITUENTS have had
TIME for COOL REFLECTION, they can
not bring themfelves to like; and have

A a   a

a RIGHT to CHOOSE others, who MAY,
if THEY PLEASE, RESCIND thefe laws,
difliked by any of their electors. But, if
a *majority* of the *new-elected* reprefentatives,
do not agree to annul them, thofe who
fhall *continue* to difapprove the laws, are
as much bound to *obey them*, as thofe,
from whom, they receive the MOST COR-
DIAL ASSENT.

THIS, is, a DUTY which arifes, not
only from the PARTICULAR FORM of
THIS CONSTITUTION; but, from the GE-
NERAL PRINCIPLE, COMMON to ALL go-
vernments. For though OUR CONSTITU-
TION, has indeed DEFINED, WHAT PER-
SONS are to CONSTITUTE the legiflature,
—the obedience which is due, to the
MAJORITY of the TWO HOUSES, with the
CONSENT of the KING, does not arife,
either from the NATURE, or NUMBER of
the perfons, conftituting it;—but from the
VERY CIRCUMSTANCE, of it's BEING the
LEGISLATURE.

LEGISLATURE. For otherwise;—a MAJO-RITY of the WHOLE PEOPLE, either by their reprefentatives, or even in their own perfons, have NO MORE RIGHT, though they MAY have MORE POWER, to con-troul a *fingle individual;*—than *any indivi-dual* has to CONTROUL ANOTHER. How-ever EXCELLENT therefore, fuch a con-ftitution of the legiflature may be, the OBEDIENCE DUE to it, *does* NOT arife FROM THAT EXCELLENCE;—but, becaufe, from the NATURE of ALL GOVERNMENTS, however DIFFERENT in their CONSTRUC-TION, OBEDIENCE is UNIVERSALLY DUE to EVERY LEGISLATURE.

In SUCH a FORM of GOVERNMENT indeed, if, a law be propofed, by *one* part of the legiflature, the DUTY of the other TWO PARTS, is, *firft* to enquire,—whether the *propofed law* be CONSONANT with the CONSTITUTION, before they determine upon it's *expedience.* For to them, is in-

trufted

trusted the *preservation* of EVERY PART of the
CONSTITUTION; but NOT by any means to
the PEOPLE at large;—any further,—than
THEIR CHOICE of REPRESENTATIVES, has a
TENDENCY, to *that* END. And, it is by so
excellent a provision, (I mean) the *not*
allowing any OTHER APPEAL to the people, than THIS, nor any appeal from them,
but by *petitions;*—that, whilst by these
means,—a defence from OPPRESSION, is
PROVIDED FOR THE PEOPLE;—STABILI-
TY is SECURED to the GOVERNMENT.

For, whatever may be the authority, which
advances the *contrary* opinion, and however
often it may have been already, and may
again hereafter be repeated,—that the PEOPLE
of ENGLAND, have by the REVOLUTION,
-acquired,—the THREE FUNDAMENTAL
RIGHTS of " *choosing their own governors,*"
—of " *cashiering them for misconduct,*"—and,
of " *framing a new government;*"—SUCH
POSITIONS are as *false* in point of *fact,*

as

as they are *repugnant* to every *juſt concep-tion* of *ſound policy:*—if, by the *people* be meant,—the *general* BULK of the COMMU-NITY; and if the aſſertors of this doƈtrine, DO NOT MEAN THIS,—and do not moſt benevolently intend to. teach it, even to the very dregs of the people,—of which I dare to ſay, they never heard a word, 'till very lately,—they certainly mean NO-THING.

For the PEOPLE at large, had no interference whatſoever, in the SETTLEMENT made at that Æra;—NO APPEAL was made to them;—and their opinions were not ASKED. But, the REVOLUTION has indeed ESTABLISHED a PRINCIPLE, of the UTMOST IMPORTANCE, and of the HIGH-EST conſequence. Which, however it may be diſputed by the FEW, or the MANY, appears to me, to be able to ſtand like a rock, unſhaken by all the buffetings of

winds

winds and waves, amidst the most tumul-
tuous agitation of the ocean.

The PRINCIPLE, I mean, is THIS. That,
when, the EXECUTIVE POWER, which is
the ONLY ONE, which can be EXTINCT,
becomes so by INCAPACITY, ABDICA-
TION, or FORFEITURE, in *consequence* of
that power, ACTING CONTRARY to
the FUNDAMENTAL, and ESTABLISHED
PRINCIPLES of the CONSTITUTION,—
THEN,—in THAT CASE, the WHOLE POW-
ER of the GOVERNMENT, DEVOLVES upon
the TWO REMAINING BRANCHES of THE
LEGISLATURE, SO FAR indeed, and NO
FURTHER,—as to give THEM a RIGHT
to SUPPLY the VACANCY, in that PARTI-
CULAR CASE, by APPOINTING ANOTHER
EXECUTIVE POWER, in as short a time
AS POSSIBLE, and in a MANNER, as con-
sentaneous with the USUAL MODE of SUC-
CESSION, as the PARTICULAR NATURE of
the CASE, WILL ADMIT.

By

By this MOST EXCELLENT PROVISION,
—the CONSTITUTION therefore, is SE-
CURED againſt VIOLATION, from the exertion of any UNLAWFUL AUTHORITY,
in the KING, which might either alter it,
or convert it into an ABSOLUTE MONAR-
CHY;—and it is likewiſe ſhielded from the
interpoſition, of any LICENTIOUS EXER-
CISE in the PEOPLE,—which might either
deſtroy it, by ANARCHY, or change it
into a DEMOCRACY. But moreover, at
the ſame time, that this *admirable provi-
ſion,*—the eſtabliſhment of which,—we owe
to the REVOLUTION,—*produces theſe ineſtimable benefits,* by guarding againſt both
tyranny and licentiouſneſs,—it is itſelf, alſo
prevented from even *verging* towards ABUSE,
from another MOST IMPORTANT PRINCI-
PLE of the conſtitution; which, totally
PROHIBITS and PREVENTS, the EXERCISE
of any SUCH power, in the *ordinary* VA-
CANCY of the throne by DEATH. For it
DOES NOT even ADMIT of the IDEA, of

SUCH

SUCH a VACANCY;—but MAINTAINS,—that the KING NEVER DIES,—or,—in other words,—that, the THRONE IS NEVER VACANT; whilft, an HEREDITARY SUCCESSOR, in a CERTAIN LINE EXISTS.

From thefe premifes, then, it neceffarily follows, that WHOEVER maintains, in *general* terms, that the PEOPLE have, in any SUCH CASES, the RIGHT of CASHIERING their governors, and of CHOOSING *other* governors,—and of FORMING what government they pleafe,—muft, upon this moft important event, either manifeft the GROSSEST DECEPTION, in the affertors themfelves.—or,—which,—I am fure, I do not believe to have been the cafe,—betray in them, the MOST CRIMINAL INTENTION, to DECEIVE others.

SUCH is the PROVISION, which our admirable *conftitution*, has framed to fecure LIBERTY to the PEOPLE, and STABILITY

to

to the GOVERNMENT. To which ends, the
RIGHTS, which the PEOPLE POSSESS,—the
POWERS which they EXERCISE,—the LI-
MITS, in which, they are CONFINED, and,
—the OBLIGATION, by which,—they are
BOUND to OBEY the LAWS,—are EQUAL-
LY CONDUCIVE. ·

That under *such* a *constitution*, men according to their different degrees of knowledge, and extent of their capacities, MAY
OFTEN DIFFER IN OPINION, concerning
the *tendency* of a law, as to the *general
good* of the *governed*, or it's *consistency* with
the *principles* of our *particular form* of
government,—can excite no surprise. But to
hear it asserted,—as we often do,—that,—
there can be *no good constitution* of government,—where,—the *people* themselves
do not give *their assent* to the laws, which
they are bound to obey;—and,—to be almost deafened, by the sounds of the NA-
TURAL RIGHTS of men, which contain,

B b   *two*

two incompatible ideas ;—muſt neceſſarily aſto-
niſh every man,—who does not YIELD to
WORDS, inſtead of ARGUMENTS,—and, who
does not miſtake, VULGAR OPINIONS, for
DEMONSTRATED TRUTHS. . For who, that
has at all exerciſed his INTELLECT in
inveſtigations, into the NATURE of MAN,
but, muſt ſee, that *ſuch doctrines*, have not
the *ſlighteſt* foundations to reſt upon, in
HUMAN NATURE? And, can *ſuch* a man,
though poſſeſſed of the greateſt candour,—
deem the publiſhers, and diſſeminators of
ſuch opinions, to be any other, than the
moſt ſuperficial of readers, and the moſt
unqualified of writers ;—as men,—who content themſelves, with the peruſal of treatiſes
upon POLITICS, merely for the ſake of
ſpouting in converſation, or, of manufacturing a book for the public ;—as men,—
who have aſſumed the taſk of teaching
others, what they themſelves had never
learned ;—as men,—who might have read
politics FOR AN AMUSEMENT,—but who
had

had never received the aid of a single
ray of judgment, reasoning, or thought,
to guide them in their enquiry into it,
AS A SCIENCE;—as men therefore,—guilty
of the highest presumption, conceit, and
arrogance,—in DICTATING,—(whilst, they
were thus IGNORANT, of the VERY FIRST
PRINCIPLES of LEGISLATION,)—LAWS to
LEGISLATORS;—and lastly as men,—*some
of whom*, are chargeable, either with the
most confirmed folly, or the highest criminality, for their ignorance, or contempt
of the DUTY of SUBJECTS, by frequently
uttering threats (if all their wishes be not
gratified) of overthrowing;—and rejoicing
by anticipation, in the destruction, of that
government,—to which, they owe the
greatest gratitude for it's past indulgencies,
and which is entitled, to their sincerest
affection, and highest reverence, for the
meekness and mildness, with which it bears
their utmost virulence of abuse,—upon every

B b 2   part

part,—both of it's CIVIL, and ECCLE-
SIASTICAL CONSTITUTION.

Those likewise, who have REALLY STU-
DIED POLITICS AS A SCIENCE, must also
be surprifed, and aftonifhed at the abfurdity, which they every day fee, of fome
men, who perhaps, would condemn *adora-
tion* of GOD, as SUPERSTITION, and HO-
MAGE to the KING, as flavery; yet,
boafting of themfelves, and glorying in
being the *mere echoes*, of fome *few individuals*, or the bigotted tools of fome party:—Of even others taking pride, and af-
fuming confequence to themfelves, from
being enlifted under the banners of one
or other of THOSE DIVISIONS, which are
not denominated, by any appellation, which
marks out any conformity with their fentiments, or fuitablenefs to their opinions;
—but, only—by the *mean* and *contemptible terms* of *reproach*,—WHIGS and TO-
RIES.

To

To every man, who at all reflects, on
the NATURE of OUR CONSTITUTION;
PRIDE or SELF-COMPLACENCY, or even
SELF-APPROBATION, derived from such no-
minal distinctions as these, must appear
to him, to be as perfectly ridiculous, as
they would be in men, who were delight-
ed with the appellation,—of MY LORD;—
when it was only a *vulgar* NICKNAME
given to them,—because,—they were *crook-
backed.*

EACH of these parties, indeed boast,
that THEY are the ONLY REAL PATRI-
OTS, and TRUE LOVERS of their country;
and each on the contrary, CONDEMN
their opponents, as it's very worst foes,
and bitterest enemies.

But, that not either of them is, more
deserving of the former appellations, than
the other, is clearly evident from this
circumstance; that however *different* may
be

be their colours,—yet, *both* are dreſſed in *liveries*, and both therefore exhibit the *badges* of their *ſlavery*.

For notwithſtanding, the vaunted, vaſt *redundance* of *modern light*, I muſt confeſs, I can *not ſee*, how any men can with juſtice, be called *true patriots and livers* of *their country*, who are *not* ſincerely attached to IT'S LAWS, and the WHOLE of it's CONSTITUTION. Certainly therefore, THOSE can not merit thoſe titles, who from their predilections, for *different* and *oppoſite parts* of it, would *hazard*, the *deſtruction* of THE WHOLE. Conſequently likewiſe, therefore not THOSE, who in their parti-coloured clothes, are each eagerly watching oppoſite ſcales, that they may ſeize an opportunity of throwing an *additional* weight, into that of their favourite ſide; and by that means make it to preponderate. But it appears to me, that they only are entitled to thoſe moſt honourable

nourable appellations, who , being attached
to *no party*, *really admire* the perfect æqui-
librium of the prefent oppofite weights;
and watch with anxiety, left even the mi-
nuteft thing; any, even the lighteft parti-
cle of duft, fhould be thrown into either;
.—which, alone would be fufficient, to give
a partial inclination to either fide, of fo nicely a polifhed beam, vibrating upon it's
centre of motion, at the flighteft touch.

But, perhaps it will be afked;—how, the
foregoing *opinions*, which have been fhown
to be *thus inconfiftent* with REASON, and
TRUE SCIENCE,—could poffibly at any
time, fpring up in the world. And how
more efpecially, could they be fo abun-
dantly propagated, and cherifhed in an
age,—in which, numbers of writers, com-
pliment their cotemporaries, and indeed it
muft be confeffed, at the fame time themfelves; by blazoning it forth, as the *wifeft*,
and moft *enlightened* age, which ever adorned

ed the annals of this nation, or even, ever illuminated this terreftrial hemifphere?

Fully, to give an anfwer to this queftion, would require an accurate inveftigation, of the *growth* and *progrefs* of literature in *this century*,—as connefted,—with the *foregoing*. An inveftigation, to which, if leifure be allowed me, I may perhaps, *hereafter*, give fome attention, as it has, no very diftant connefìtion, with, " AN EN-" QUIRY INTO THE IMPEDIMENTS TO HU-" MAN KNOWLEDGE." A fubjeft which, *very* early in life engaged my enquiries, and which, for almoft thirty years, has never ceafed altogether to be, the objeft, of my inveftigation.

But, to affign *fome* of the *proximate* caufes, is not at any time very difficult; and may now, perhaps, be attended with fome benefit.

Firft,

First, then;—becaufe,—moft of the governments of *Europe*, in which, *fcience* flourifhes, have been *monarchies*, and not *republics*.

Few *political* writers therefore, have confidered the *various inconveniences*, which muft neceffarily be involved in *every plan* devifed, and executed, by fuch fallible creatures, as *men*; and fome of which, though different in *kind*, muft therefore appertain to *every* fpecies of government. For this reafon then, it was natural for politicians, more attentively to mark, and more accurately to defcribe, the inconveniences produced by *that form* of government, under which they lived, and of which, they had actual experience, than thofe evils, which, exifting under conftitutions; to which they were ftrangers, could only be made known to them, by vague reports, and difputable information. Hence then, it neceffarily follows, from a principle common to the *fen-*

C c   *fes,*

fes, the *imagination*, and the *intellect* ;—that the one set of objects, because near, would appear enlarged beyond their real dimensions; and the others would be represented, as diminished even to miniatures. A line therefore, in the second satire of Horace, will inform us, why under these circumstances, men would *hastily* wish to live in a state, which really approaches in the next degree, to NO GOVERNMENT at all; rather, than to remain the subjects of a government, which may be classed under any SPECIES of MONARCHY. The line begins,—*Dum vitant, &c.*—But,—VERBUM; SAT SAPIENTI.

Secondly, because,—in early youth, all our ideas of LIBERTY, are so associated with the *republican form* of government; and we are then so captivated, with the gay and gaudy colours of the eloquence, with which they are tinted;—that,—even,
—when

—when we are MEN, we are not *willing*
to reflect, upon the evils, which, they produced; and of which, a very flight attention to the faithful records of hiftory;
would give us a full, but melancholy conviction.

For, if we mark with any obfervation,
the hiftory of the REPUBLIC of ATHENS,
we fhall find,—that the adjudications of the
people, were, for the moft part, denun-
ciations of vengeance, againft thofe great
men, who had rendered the moft effential
fervices to the ftate; and who by their
wifdom, and *virtue*, reflect the higheft honour upon themfelves, and their country.

So likewife, if we recollect, the rife,
the progrefs, and declenfion of the people
of ROME;—we fhall difcover,—that, having
been fafcinated, by the *external* fplendor
of the ftate, during the times of the republic; we had forgotten the perpetual, *in-*

C c 2

ternal

ternal diffenfions, by which it was con-
ſtantly agitated. And, ſtruck with horror,
at ſome particularly flagrant acts of wick-
ednefs, committed by ſome of thoſe wretch-
es, who, though ROMAN EMPERORS, were
the vileſt of the human ſpecies,—and *blots*
on human nature;—that we had buried in
oblivion,—the contentions,—wars,—proſcrip-
tions,—and maſſacres,—which, though more
horrible in their effects, and more extenfive in their operations, were perpetrated,
during the continuance of the ſtate, under
the FORM of a REPUBLIC.

Thirdly, becauſe, though the TRUE DOC-
TRINE, of the UNIVERSAL DUTY OF SUB-
JECTS TO OBEY THEIR GOVERNORS, has
been frequently maintained; yet,—it was
upon WRONG PRINCIPLES only, that it has
been hitherto defended.

For, nothing is more common, in the
progreſſions of ſcience, than to behold,

TRUE

TRUE OPINIONS *admitted* in *one age*,—though
fupported by BAD ARGUMENTS;—and the
fame true opinions, rejected in the NEXT,
only becaufe, they had not *before* been
founded upon *juft principles.* And on the
contrary, it is not lefs frequent, to fee
opinions, received, from the fuppofed *ftrength*
of the proofs, by which, they are prop-
ped;—when,—upon a *further* examination,
—THOSE VERY OPINIONS, are not only
difcovered by *other* arguments to be FALSE
in THEMSELVES; but, the *proofs* alfo, which
had been applied to them, are found, to
be fo exceedingly weak, as to be totally
incapable, of fuftaining the weight, they
had been provided, to fupport.

Fourthly, becaufe, in this nation, the arguments in defence of the *conclufions,* I
have deduced, were before not only, NOT
taken from the FIRST PRINCIPLES, which
I have now drawn FRESH, I truft, from
the WELL of TRUTH, and from which, as

a

a GENERAL SOURCE,—ALL *governments*, I have fhown, originally flow. But *thofe principles* which had been produced by others, were not only extremely impure in themfelves, but were likewife rendered *putrid*, by a mixture of certain *phlogiftic* ideas, of the *nature* of government in GENERAL, and of *our* OWN CONSTITUTION in PARTICULAR;—fuch as the JUS DIVINUM, and HEREDITARY INDEFEASIBLE RIGHTS of KINGS, &c. Evident however as this is, —numbers perhaps, enveloped as they are in *prejudices*, will obftinately REJECT MINE too, AS UNWHOLESOME,—without employing even either their eyes, or their tafte, in the ATTEMPT TO DISCOVER, how totally *they* differ from thofe, which they have formerly reprobated, and long fince regorged.

Fifthly, becaufe, even, the PRINCIPLES of the REVOLUTION, have been by many, if not by moft men, totally mifunderftood. For

For *that event*, has been generally imagined, if not univerfally believed, to have
fprung from the RIGHTS, COMMON to ALL
MANKIND; under EVERY SPECIES, and
FORM of government. From this miftake
therefore, Sir, of your *mafter*, Mr. Locke,
and your other teachers, who were *firft*
his pupils, that event, has been repeated-
ly cited, and reiteratedly boafted of, not
only as a LESSON, but alfo an EXAMPLE
of INSTRUCTION, to ALL OTHER NATI-
ONS. It having been conftantly pointed
out to *other* ftates, as an objeft of IMI-
TATION, for the conduft, THEY OUGHT
to purfue, whenever the emotions of the
governed, fhall be in difcord, with the
fentiments of the governors. Whereas, in
reality,—the PRINCIPLES of the *revolution*,
were only a GLORIOUS MANIFESTATION,
of the PARTICULAR RIGHTS of BRITONS:
(fo far as I have above explained THEM
to extend)—IMPARTED, by the LAWS,—
and

and ſtrengthened by the PECULIAR FRAME, —of the ENGLISH CONSTITUTION.

Sixthly, there were, TWO OTHER CAU-SES, which occaſioned a very ready ad-miſſion, and general reception to the doc-trines, oppoſite to thoſe, which I have been introducing, and ſupporting. *Theſe are*, the almoſt univerſal paſſions, of PRIDE and AMBITION; though the one, is ſome-times cloathed, even in the plain garb of humility, and the other, often retires far diſtant, from courts and palaces.

For, as I have before obſerved, the VERY SAME PASSIONS,—which,—PROMPT men,—*when*, in POWER,—to become TY-RANTS;—INSTIGATE likewiſe the SAME, or OTHER MEN,—*when*,—OUT OF POWER, —to turn REBELS.

It is evident therefore, that from the prevalence of theſe two paſſions, NO DOC-

TRINES

TRINE's could be more acceptable, to the
MAJORITY of mankind, than the notions,
with which, LOCKE, and *other writers*
upon government, have flattered them;—
I mean,—in refpect to their PERFECT
ORIGINAL EQUALITY with *thofe*, who, are
now by their rank *elevated* above, and by
their power, are placed in *authortiy* over
them. This pofition, muft in itfelf alone,
have afforded them great fatisfaction. But,
the INFERENCE, which, they could not
fail to draw from the premifes,—prompted
as they were, by the paffions of human
nature,—muft have imparted to them, a
ftill greater pleafure. For the deduction
from hence, was fo obvious, that they
could not poffibly overlook it, efpecially,
when inftigated by *pride* and *ambition*;
and therefore they immediately, and indeed, fuppofing the truth of the pofition,
—very juftly inferred,—that the only *pro-*
per reform in ALL governments,—is,—to
RESTORE that PRISTINE ftate of things,—

either

either altogether, or at least so far,—as
THEIR OWN CLASSES ARE CONCERNED,
and all others are affected, who hold those
political tenets; which, whoever can re-
peat by *rote*, is deemed to be, as com-
pleat in ALL WISDOM, as even the STO-
ICS WISE MAN; and as SUPEREMINENT
in GOODNESS, as that CHRISTIAN PHILO-
SOPHER,—who, *Pope* says,—was possessed,
of "*every virtue under heaven.*"

From these notions however, it must
be confessed, there arises such an idea of
their own *self-importance*, and *dignity* of
character in adopting them, and such a
full blown conceit, of their own SUPERI-
OR WISDOM, and of their own UNPA-
RALLELED VIRTUE in maintaining them;
—that the flame of ambition, sometimes
breaks forth into open view: And these
philosophers, as they boast themselves to
be,—can not sometimes forbear, even in
defiance of prudence, to BETRAY their

EXPECTATION,

EXPECTATION,—that notwithſtanding, they may at *firſt* endeavour to RAISE:—They HOPE however, SOON AGAIN to DISPERSE, this *rain-bowed—coloured bubble,* of EQUALITY.

For, conſtant experience teaches us, that there is not ANY CLASS of men, who, under the *preſent* exiſting governments, are ſo tenacious of their *real* rank, as theſe ADVOCATES for EQUALITY, are of their *fancied* one; which in their own eſtimation, they not only appreciate as due to their worth; but which, they on all occaſions, with no little anxiety to themſelves, and inconvenience to others, aſſume;—contrary to all the rules of law,—cuſtom,—preſcription,— courteſy,—and good manners. THEY, truly,—*diſdain* to ſhow any reſpect to TITLES;—they pay their homage,—only to MERIT; and being in *their own* opinion, poſſeſſed of a *monopoly* of all the WISDOM, and VIRTUE in the world, they very eaſily conclude, that

D d 2   THEY

THEY are THEMSELVES ALONE, ENTITLED
to the very HIGHEST RANK. So incauti-
ous are they from confidence, or so ignorant are they of mankind, as to imagine;
—that other men, will believe them to be
the SINCERE advocates, for an EQUALITY
of CONDITIONS; becaufe,—they fhow that
they HATE *that* rank and power in *others*,
which, *they do not themfelves* POSSESS; though
whatever privilege or *authority*, they *may
happen* TO HAVE, they convert into *tyranny* over thofe, who *have* it *not*.

If therefore, by ftepping forth as *pretended champions*, for an *equality* of ranks,
they could *really overturn*, the prefent eftablifhed fyftems of government;—with all
the rafh inexperience of PHAETON, they
fancy,—they fhould foon feat themfelves
in the chariot, and direct the horfes of the
fun;—and with all *his* blind confidence,
they imagine, they fhould then glorioufly
illuminate, the whole fyftem of the world.
Though

Though better would it be for *them now,*
as it would *before* have been likewife, for
their *kindred-minded philofophers* in FRANCE,
—to be *warned,*—rather by *his example;*—
than fired by his *ambition.* Left it fhould
be thought neceffary, that *they,* like *him,*—
fhould be deftroyed by lightning;—as the
only refource left,—for the prefervation of
all the other regions of the earth, from a
general conflagration.

I muft however, do thefe gentlemen the
juftice to confefs, that there is *another confequence* of the paffions, which, are the *caufes,*
of their blind credulity, in the *belief* of
their political doctrines,—their pertinacious
bigotry in the affertion of them,—and their
rooted antipathy to all who oppofe them,
—which they have never difcerned, and
of which, therefore, they are totally un-
confcious.

For

For it is evident, that exactly in proportion as *such doctrines*, are adapted, to
gratify the paſſions I have juſt mentioned,
—they muſt in the generality. of mankind,
—neceſſarily *excite emotions* of *pleaſure* and
delight.

But however, well acquainted theſe *profound politicians*, may be, with the analyſis
of the particles of bodies;—yet, as they
are perfectly unpracticed, in the analyſation
of the ſentiments of the mind;—and but
very little accuſtomed, even to the PER-
CEPTION of .TRUTH;—they muſt therefore,
neceſſarily MISTAKE in *this* inſtance, which
the *unreflecting multitude* do in *all* .caſes,—
the PLEASURABLE EBULLITIONS ariſing,
from. the PASSIONS,—for,—the INTELLEC-
TUAL EMOTIONS, which in reality, belong
only, to the DEMONSTRATION of SCIENCE.

And, hence it is, that we ſo often hear
them, vaunting of their RATIONAL NOTI-
ONS,

ONS, and LIBERAL OPINIONS;—whilſt they themſelves, are totally ignorant of their *true origin*, and *real ſource*.—For, it is evident, that, *the former epithet*, can not, by any means, belong to *their* notions or their opinions,—as ariſing, from a *deep* enquiry into the FIRST PRINCIPLES,—and an *accurate* examination of the PRIMARY DEFINITION,—upon which,—they are founded; and from which, they are deduced, by a nice, and accurate concatenation of proofs; —which,—is the ONLY PROCESS,—by which,—ANY *notions*, can poſſibly have a *legitimate* claim, to the *title* of RATIONAL. This is manifeſt, from this plain and well known faſt, that at the very moment, they are boaſting of their *ſuperior* powers of *reaſoning*, they are almoſt always betraying the lamentable poverty, and miſerable emptineſs, of their argumentative ſtores. As indeed, almoſt every *ſingle page*, of *theſe letters, ſufficiently proves.*

So

So likewife, in reference to the LIBE-
RALITY, of their notions or opinions, it
is *equally manifeft*, that they can not fet up
their claim to *this* title, from *their liberality* of fentiments, towards thofe, who differ from them. Nor, from *their freedom*
from *prejudices*, either *againft other* men's
opinions, or in *favour of their own*. Becaufe, whilft they are in the very aft of
boafting, of the *liberality* of *their* own fentiments, they are frequently, at the very in-
ftant, fo *grofsly abufing*, that CIVIL and RELI-
GIOUS ESTABLISHMENT, to which, they are
themfelves indebted, for *toleration* and *protection;* fo as to leave us totally at a lofs
to determine, which, is the moft wonderful;—the FORBEARANCE of the one party,
or the INGRATITUDE of the other. In
one refpect however, the conduct of the
latter, is perfectly confiftent, and their affertions are equally true. For, whilft they
reprefent the doctrines of their opponents,
as fo *abhorrent* from REASON, and COM-

MON

MON SENSE, that they need NO REFU-
TATION; they COMMAND the world, upon
their IPSE DIXIT, to BELIEVE; that *their*
OWN OPINIONS, are fo SELF-EVIDENT, as
to REQUIRE NO ARGUMENT, for *their*
fupport.

Thefe are facts, which have likewife been
in no fmall degree apparent, in the courfe
of THESE LETTERS; but the reader can
only fee them in their brighteft colours,
and their really gigantic dimenfions, by a
careful infpection, of thefe authors OWN
WRITINGS.

Thefe circumftances, then, afford *another*
proof, of the truth of my foregoing pofition,—that,—the CAUSES of their other
erroneous opinions, and of their fancied
fuperiority, in *rational* and *liberal* notions,
can only, really originate from the operations,—though as I am ready to allow,
unperceived by themfelves,—of pride, va-

E e   nity,

nity, and ambition. And indeed, I am extremely glad, that TRUTH warrants this conclusion. For I would much rather, impute their miftakes to a *neglected education*, than to any *original inferiority*, in their under-ftandings.

Impelled therefore, by thefe emotions, or paffions, moft gladly, would they af-fume the government, of *all* the kingdoms of the earth. But as unfortunately for them, not even the empire over *one* of them, *as*, they are *now conftituted*, is *likely* to fall to their fhare;—the *next degree* of *pleafure*, which they can receive;—is,— from STRIPPING *governors*, as much as they can, of all *power* of *controul* over THEM, AS SUBJECTS. For, *this* they know, would not only in the *next* degree, beft gratify their inclinations, but may perhaps, —they think,—pave the way in time,—to *their own* acquifiton of power, and autho-rity;—and therefore, they term all thefe

levelling

levelling-principles, not only the *most*, but the *only* RATIONAL NOTIONS of government.

Of the EFFECTS of such principles, we may see the PROOFS in the *philosophers* in FRANCE, who loudly also pleaded, for an EQUALITY of conditions.—But who likewise we find, by no means, intended to *humble themselves*, to the rank of those, who were *before* in the classes *below* THEM;—and thus by sharing, to alleviate *their* burthens.—No far from it.—For *this* they knew, would be to imbibe the *true spirit*, of that *detestable superstition*,—as they term it, which others call CHRISTIANITY. But, in conformity with the *more enlightening inspiration* of PHILOSOPHY; they as soon as possible, hurled from their seats,—ALL THOSE,—who had been *before* elevated *above* THEM,—that they might partake, of the plunder of their power, and their wealth;—and thus, have forced themselves,

E e 2 —for

—for a time at leaſt, by *art*,—into a height,—far above· *that* LEVEL,—to which, by the properties, given to them by nature, they are fitted to riſe; and to which, they muſt again by the laws of gravity, ſoon, once more ſink.

So alſo, in reſpect to their *religious* opinions. Finding that they have *no* probability at preſent, of *eſtabliſhing their own*; —as the *next* ſtep, which would be moſt acceptable to them, they endeavour to perſuade the world, that the TRUTH or NATURE of any *particular* religion, or, the ſentiments of it's *various ſects*, have not the REMOTEST CONNECTION, with the HAPPINESS of the STATE; and that, as *religion*, is of NO USE in CONDUCING· to CIVIL HAPPINESS; it OUGHT to have no kind of INFLUENCE upon it, whatſoever. And conſequently therefore, that the LEGISLATURE has NO RIGHT to INTERMEDDLE in it's concerns, nor even to
THINK

THINK of any means, which may conduce
to it's ESTABLISHMENT, or PROPAGA-
TION.

From hence then, it follows, in their
opinion;· that,—NO MAN'S NOTIONS ·or
·ACTIONS, are REALLY ᴌ LIBERAL, who
treat,—with the *utmoſt candour, mildneſs,
forbearance,* and *brotherly charity,*—ALL who
differ from *him ever ſo much,* in RELIGI-
OUS SFNTIMENTS;—but, that HE is the
only truly liberal man, who, with the *utmoſt
violence, virulence,* and even ungentleman-
like licentiouſneſs, vilifies ALL, who, *will not*
MAINTAIN with THEM,—that men's *noti-
ons* of religion, are matters ·of PERFECT
·INDIFFERENCE, to the WELFARE of· so-
CIETY.

The . CONSEQUENCES, which NECESSA-
RILY follow, from theſe brilliant ideas of
rationality and *liberality,* if *rightly* drawn
out to their CONCLUSIONS;—are evident-
ly

ly the following, which, whilſt theſe writers are *out* of *power* themſelves, they wiſh to ſee eſtabliſhed.

Firſt. That, the moſt RATIONAL and LIBERAL government, *is that*, in which *each* man, is *ſolely his own governor;*—or in other words,—THAT STATE, is the BEST GOVERNED, WHICH HAS NO GO-VERNMENT.

Secondly. That the MOST RATIONAL and LIBERAL of ALL RELIGIONS,—*is that,*—which admits of of the MOST INDIFFERENCE to it's PRECEPTS; and has LEAST INFLU-ENCE upon *men*, *as* MEMBERS of *ſociety;* —or in other words,—that a RELIGION, is *then* MOST BENEFICIAL TO A STATE, when, it HAS LEAST INFLUENCE.

ANOTHER CAUSE—of the *prevalence* of *ſuch* doctrines, is,—becauſe, in reali-ty, the TRUE CHARACTERISTICS of the

CONCLUSION of this VERY ENLIGHTEN-
ED EIGHTEENTH CENTURY,—are NOT
what thefe writers fuppofe,—and what, for
the gratification of their own vanity,—they
wifh others to believe.—But on the con-
trary, they confift in *faɛ̃*,—in the ENOR-
MOUS NUMBER of it's VORACIOUS REA-
DERS;—in the great ABUNDANCE of it's
MULTIFARIOUS WRITERS;—and in the
MULTITUDE of it's FLUENT SPEAKERS.
And, at the fame time alfo,—in it's WOE-
FUL PAUCITY of DEEP THINKERS;—SA-
GACIOUS INVESTIGATORS;—and ORIGI-
NAL GENIUSES. Thefe are clearly eviden-
ced by it's boldnefs, and confidence in
ASSERTION, it's weaknefs and incapacity
in ARGUMENT. It's prefumption and con-
ceit, in fuppofing itfelf to be irradiated
with the brighteft light, when at the fame
time, even a very weak one, is too ftrong
for it's very feeble optics.

For

For in proportion, as the acquifition of OPINIONS, has been facilitated, the attainment of KNOWLEDGE, has been diminifhed. As men, have had *more volumes* TO READ, they have devoted a *lefs portion of their time* to STUDY. As BOOKS, have increafed in NUMBERS, REASONING has decreafed in ACUTENESS. And of all the phænomena, which this age has exhibited, in the regions of literature;—TWO will appear the MOST REMARKABLE, and WONDERFUL to future times; if there fhould arife an able and impartial critic, to trace the *rife, progrefs,* and *declenfion* of IT's OPINIONS. •

Firft. That thofe authors,—who WROTE the MOST,—THOUGHT the LEAST.

Secondly. That thofe, who made the *loudeft claims* to the GREATEST RATIONALITY, or to the HIGHEST POWERS OF REASONING; were the LEAST ELEVATED

above

above others, by *this* CHARACTERISTIC of man; and muſt, in the next century,—for the *very ſhort* time,—that any obſcure veſtige of their memory, ſhall be traced, —be ranked amongſt ſome of the *lower claſſes*, of the *worſt reaſoners*, of *any* age.

So well founded, do theſe poſitions appear to me, that I dare, *here*, to make the appeal to the *judgment* of POSTERI-TY; and even to call for your own writings, Sir, to be the evidence produced, upon which, the ſentence of acquittal, or condemnation, ſhould be paſſed.

When however, I am appreciating the literature of the age, I hope, I ſhall not be underſtood, as ſpeaking of the *whole* Iſland of Great-Britain; but only of this *ſouthern* part of it. For I have before acknowledged, in reſpect to our united brethren in the north, without aſſuming

F f

the

the arduous office of a reviewer, in determining upon the *truth*, or *falfehood* of
their opinions;—that we certainly *there*
find writers, poffeffed of DEEP THOUGHT,
CLOSE INVESTIGATION, and BRILLIANT
POWERS. Nor, when confined even within *thefe* bounds, do I hope, to be underftood, as meaning to characterife the WHOLE
of *this century*. For certainly, *confidered*
as an WHOLE; *it* will ftand VERY HIGH
in the annals of fame. .Nor likewife, would
I be underftood, to include *all* the authors, who now write towards it's clofe.
For the name, of *Mr. Burke* can not fail,
to occur to every one's recollection; and
no one indeed, can be fo ignorant, as not
to know, that there are likewife feveral other
very ingenious writers, now living; though
it would be an invidious, and odious tafk
in an individual, to enumerate their names.
Men, who,—notwithftanding the difcourage-
ments *they* have received, and every man
of

of real genius, muft receive, from partial criticifm at prefent;—will, from their various purfuits, be ranked in *future times*, amongft fome of the *bright* ornaments, of the literature of this country.

But, my intention is only, *more particularly* to *characterife* T H O S E ;—who,—by forming themfelves into parties, and uniting into cabals,—ftrengthen their own confidence in themfelves, and by mutual puffing each other, are fo inflated with inflammable air, as to imagine, that they are able to foar like balloons, to the fublimeft heights. And as the *vulgar,* whether, they be called the learned, or are truly denominated the unlearned, always miftake *affertions* for *proofs,* they readily give credit to *their own accounts* of *each other,* and hence, they become the writers, who are at *prefent,* the moft heard of,—moft talked of,—moft quoted, —and moft flattered.

F f 2   It.

It is from fuch inſtances only, I mean to *infer*, that the *concluſion* of this century, does *not* furpaſs the *foregoing*, nor by any means, *equal* it's own commencement. For, though many more as I have already faid, are certainly now become readers, and writers, than there were formerly;—yet,—as they are not on *that* account, DEEPER THINKERS, and BETTER REASONERS,— the POPULARITY of any OPINION, can be NO PROOF of it's TRUTH.

There is indeed, one melancholy inſtance of neglected learning and ability, which will juſtly brand this age, with the fevere cenſure of poſterity; and of which, numbers muſt partake, who are not circumſcribed within that narrow circle, of which I have juſt now, been drawing a defcription. I mean, FLOYER SYDENHAM: That moſt learned tranſlator, and moſt philofophical annotator, upon *fome* of the *dialogues*, of
                                    the

the *illuſtrious Plato*. But, ſo little was the *taſte* of the age ſuited, either to the inva-luable works of the author, or the incom-parable notes of the tranſlator, that the latter I underſtand,—died, on account of debt, in a common jail; WHO,—in any *for-mer* age, in which, ALL MEN HIGH IN OF-FICE, eſteemed it their own higheſt honour, to patronize *genius* and *learning*,—would have acquired, what he was juſtly entitled to,—both, *wealth* and *honours*.

In ALL the LIBERAL and MECHANIC ARTS, there can be no doubt, but that this age *far* outſhines any, which Britain has ever ſeen. In painting in particular, the genius of a REYNOLDS alone, darting it's rays, both from his *works*, and his *diſ-. courſes*, diffuſes a luſtre around it's cloſe, far brighter than the meridian ſplendour of any former century.

In

In *electricity*, *magnetifm*, *chemiftry*, *&c.* it certainly has to boaft, a large collection of *facts*, eftablifhed upon well-inftitued *experiments*: which, may perhaps fupply another. *Newton*, with many materials for a future fyftem. And fo far, Sir, as you have had your fhare, in contributing, to the collection

—— *Sume Superbiam*
Quæfitam meritis.

Laftly, then;—for *this*, follows as a *confequence* from the *preceding* reafon; many mere momentary meteors, are in the literary hemifphere at prefent, miftaken for planets,—and planets for fixed ftars. Confequently therefore, the *mafs* of the *people*, conceiving the rays, which are merely reflected from the *moon*, to be the *direct* beams iffuing from the *fun*;—they are incapable of diftinguifhing, the fhades of
bodies

bodies from their outlines, and miftake what are only fhadows, for real obje6s.

Thus, Sir, (to borrow your well-known metaphor) I have now layed, and fet fire to a train, which has entirely blown up, ONE of your PRINCIPAL FORTS, from it's very foundations: and which has likewife, *already undermined* the OTHER: Though towards *that*,—*this* train, was not indeed, immediately dire6ted, in a ftrait line. As to any mufquetry, therefore, which you may have drawn up around you, as a guard to your own perfon; *thefe*, even your prudence and compaffion fhould have fpared; inftead of betraying your own im-becility, by expofing thofe, to certain de-ftru6tion, who are both too weak to refift an adverfary, and too feeble to annoy him.

The firing a volley at THEM, can only be confidered, as *a feu de joie*, after the victory.

victory. For, their powder, has, during the
fiege, loft all it's force, if it ever had any;
and even the locks of their mufquets,
which were at firft, extremely weak and
ill conftructed, are moft of them now,—
even fhattered into pieces.

' I am, Sir,

Yours, &c.

LETTER

LETTER X.

SIR,

WHEN inſtead of advancing, I reſt upon my arms, and look back, upon the deveſtation, and demolition, which the irreſiſtible force of my battery has produced,—and ſee numbers, already weeping over the ſcattered fragments, and deſolated ruins of your *principal fort :*—PITY, prompts in me the wiſh, to ſlacken my career, and even, to deſiſt, from further triumph. It urges me, to refrain from adding, to the number of the conquered,

G g   and

and to fpare the weaknefs, of the few of your forces, which ftill remain.

But, when it occurs to my recolleﬅion, that to a *foldier*,—CONTEMPT, is WORSE than DEATH;—it feems to me, moﬅ probable,—that the fame fentiments are entertained by all, who are engaged in any other fpecies of POLEMICKS; and then, even compaffion teaches me, that it is more merciful to kill, than to fave.

As therefore, you have arranged in fome order, fome few of your rank and file, which are ftill left: I fhall employ a few minutes more, in advancing againﬅ *them*. For though it is true, that none of them, were firﬅ inlifted, and trained by *you*, but, are only fome infirm, old troops, whom you picked up, from other generals, I fhall now prefent them, with a few vollies of fmall arms; leﬅ, *weak* as they are, they fhould, as I have faid, deem the paffing

them

them by unnoticed, as a greater difgrace; and which confequently, they would be much lefs willing to fuftain, than to be covered with wounds, or left dead in the field.

I fhall therefore hold no further parley, but immediately proceed to difperfe, the feeble body, of light-armed troops, which you have ftationed, in the *third letter*, *page* 22.

The *firft* pofition you have taken, is this,—" that the REVOLUTION in this coun-
" try, is an EVENT, which, *more* than *any*
" *thing* elfe, has *opened* the eyes of Eng-
" lifhmen, to the *true principles* of *govern-*
" *ment.*

Now, Sir, by thofe, to *whom,* the revolution ferved in your opinion, as a fubftitute for the operation of couching, I conclude, that you muft moft affuredly mean

G g 2   yourfelf,

yourſelf, and your friends. For you certainly will not allow, that *any others*, *do*
underſtand the *true principles*, of government.
But, as I have already, I do not ſcruple
to ſay, DEMONSTRATED, that *they* are the
very perſons, who have more *particularly*
MISUNDERSTOOD, the *true principles* of
that EVENT, as well as, THE FIRST *principles of* ALL GOVERNMENT; it follows,
—that in this caſe,—" the *blind are* led
" by the *blind;"*—and if therefore, they
have had their eyes opened at all,—it can
have really ſerved to no other purpoſe,—
than to make, their,—" *darkneſs viſible.*"—
But, as I have now in this work, erected,
and lighted up ſo many beacons, for our
guidance and ſecurity, I do not entertain
the ſlighteſt apprehenſion,—for the *laſting*
peace, proſperity, and *happineſs,* of *theſe*
kingdoms; nor feel the leaſt atom of fear,
leſt this adumbration,—in which,—you and
your friends are envcloped,—ſhould ever
degenerate into ſuch a plague,—as that of
                                        Egypt;

Egypt;—fo that the DARKNESS, fhould not only, be " SEEN,"—but alfo,—be even,— " FELT."

That " *the great objeɛt of all government,* " *is, the* PUBLIC GOOD,—is certainly ONE of thofe undeniable truths, which fprings, from the very origin of *all* government. This I have already afferted, and did always as readily allow;—upon the CONVICTION of REASON; as *you* can poffibly have admitted it, upon your principles of AVOWED BIGOTRY, to Mr. LOCKE. But at the fame time, I have alfo fhown, that the *deduɛtions,* which HE has drawn from it, and which YOU, as the fhadow following the fubftance, likewife reprefent, are, in *direɛt oppofition* to REASON.

For, you maintain, " *that from* THIS " *principle, it follows, that all magiſtrates are* " ANSWERABLE *to the* PEOPLE, *for their* " *conduɛt in office, and* REMOVABLE *at* THEIR " PLEASURE,

" PLEASURE, *and that the* RIGHT *of* RESIST-
" ING *an oppreſſive government,* THAT IS,
" SUCH, as THE PEOPLE SHALL DEEM TO BE
" OPPRESSIVE, MUST BE HELD SACRED."

Now, Sir, THESE PREMISES, and CON-
CLUSIONS, appear to me, to be much farther diſtant from each other, than even
your reſidence at *Birmingham,* from mine
at *Great Yarmouth.* And, as you have not
been ſo kind, as to erect any of thoſe
direction-poſts, called REASONS, or ARGU-
MENTS, to point us out the road, from the
one, to the other; I ſhould no more ex-
pect, to ſet out from the *premiſes,* and ar-
rive by a *ſtrait line* at the *concluſion,* without wandering in ſcepticiſm, or plunging
into the abyſs of error; than, to ſet out
from the *latter town,* and by the *ſame
means* to reach the former, without being
drowned in a river, or foundered in a
bog.

Beſides,

Befides, in the *one* cafe, I have already fhown;—that the road is *totally obftructed,* by an *inacceffible,* and *unpaffable* mountain; which, entirely blocks up the paffage. Becaufe, from the very NATURE of ALL GOVERNMENT, it follows,—or rather,—the very *word,*—GOVERNMENT,—in itfelf,—IMPLIES,—that the GOVERNORS *of a ftate,*—are to RULE the GOVERNED;—NOT the GOVERNED, *to* RULE THE GOVERNORS.

Therefore, Sir, though *you* have been pleafed to *obferve,* in the fame leaf, and no doubt *believe,*—that the " *public good,* " being the moft NATURAL and RATIONAL " of *all rules;* and what, is MUCH MORE " EASY to DETERMINE, than either, what, " —GOD HAS ORDAINED,—or,—what AN- " TIQUITY AUTHORISES;" *true,* and *felf-evident,* as fuch pofitions may be to you, and confequently, that legiflation is the EASIEST of all tafks:—Yet, *that truth and felf-evidence, muft be totally undifcernible by me,*—

me,—'*till* you have PROVED,—that the RIGHT of the PEOPLE,—is, to have the COMMAND OVER GOVERNORS; and the DUTY of GOVERNORS, is, to pay OBEDIENCE to the PEOPLE; and alſo, that the MOST ILLITERATE OF MANKIND, CAN MUCH EASIER DISCOVER, WHAT CONDUCES TO THE PUBLIC GOOD;—THAN GOD, CAN REVEAL IT.

In page 24, you tell us, " that men " ſurely can not be ſaid to *give up* their " *natural rights*, by entering into a com- " paƈt for the better *ſecuring* of them." By which, NATURAL RIGHTS, you tell us, you mean, LIFE, LIBERTY, and PROPERTY.

This propoſition indeed, Sir, would be moſt certainly, not only *ſelf-evident*, but even *identical;* did it not, a little unfortunately TAKE for GRANTED, that there ARE SUCH THINGS, as NATURAL RIGHTS.
Now,

Now, on account of this unlucky accident, you muſt be under the unavoidable neceſ-ſity, not only of *undertaking* a taſk, but alſo of *accompliſhing* an exploit,—which,— I am afraid, is infinitely leſs ſuited to the ſtrength of your mind, than the *hardeſt* labour,—or even *all* the labours of *Her-cules* were, to the *vigour* of his body.

For, before this poſition, can poſſibly be admitted,—which indeed, you hold in common with your ſchool-maſters, though to you alone belong, the unparticipated ho-nour of ſo clear, ſo accurate, and ſo very ſenſible a ſtatement of it;—you muſt firſt DESTROY not only, the WHOLE CONCA-TENATION, but likewiſe, every *individual link* in the *chain*, of THAT REASONING,— which *holds*,—and *binds* together, the *fore-going letters*. But, as this is ſo arduous a taſk, that from fear of the accompliſh-ment, you may not be willing to ſee the neceſſity for undertaking it; or, which, for

H h   want

want of clearer logical fpe&acles, you may not be able to difcover;—permit me to exemplify it by a more familiar inftance, which, having a reference to your own perfon, may be to *you*, eafier of comprehenfion, than any other illuftration, I could poffibly produce.

Let us fuppofe then, fome one to maintain,—that *Dr. Prieftley*, has NOT *given up* all his CAPACITY for REASONING, by that portion of it, which, we find, he has *retained* in his *letters* to *Mr. Burke*.

Now certainly, no one could poffibly be fo foolifh, as to maintain, that *if* you *have* RETAINED "*a capacity for reafoning*," in thofe letters;—that you had, when writing them, either *loft it*, or *given it up*. But, ftill, there may notwithftanding, remain, *two* poffible fubjefts of *difpute*. For, it is not quite impoffible,—that fome fceptical opponent to your admirer, might DOUBT, whether

whether you *ever had*, or even DENY, that you ever HAD,—at any time,—*any capacity for reasoning;* or even, if you *had*,—whether, you *retained any*, in your *letters* to *Mr. Burke.* And after reading these letters of mine, to which *yours* gave occasion, should any one be so *whimsical*, as to demand of your admirer, PROOFS of these points; HE must necessarily *undertake the Herculean* labour, of exhibiting them, before, he could procure from the objector, any *assent*, to his *first* position. But, *with such a requisition*, it appears to me, as *difficult*, to find *any man* ABLE to COMPLY; *as* it seems *impossible*, that YOU should be *capable*, of SATISFYING the *demand*, in the *former* case;—for the sole purpose of illustrating which, I have introduced, this *latter* instance.

As to all your little poppings, in defence of the positions, which relate to the *election*, and *dethronement* of *kings*, they were

evidently

evidently charges, only of powder. For, all the ſhot, which is alone fitted for the maintenance of ſuch poſts, has been already compleatly deſtroyed, by the long train of artillery, which I arranged, oppoſite to your fort: ſo that it would now be in *me*, a criminal waſte of powder, not only to fire off a ſingle charge, but even to make your ſoldiers wink, by giving them a flaſh in the pan.

But, Sir, there is *one* paſſage in this *illuſtrious* THIRD LETTER, which, though it entirely delivers us from all employment, of the faculty of thinking, for the purpoſe of refuting it; and affords us the moſt *entire diſpenſation*, from all *inveſtigation*, by offering us only, what we have hundreds of times before, both read, heard, reprobated, and deſpiſed; yet,—I can not paſs it by unnoticed; as it gave birth to a reflection, which was to me attended with great pain, though the relation of it,

may

may perhaps, to others, be followed by much benefit.

For, it gave *me* reafon to lament, that notwithftanding, the vaft *labour* you have employed, in *putting together,* fuch a *multiplicity* of *books,* as, you *have already* FABRICATED, that, you had not, *before* the publication of your letters to *Mr. Burke,* *added* to THEM, *one labour more.* The tafk, I mean,—of *making* an ENGLISH DICTIONARY; for the *benefit* of *yourfelf,* and of *your friends.* For, by *this omiffion,* you have moft unluckily *puzzled yourfelf,* and *them,* as to the *meaning* of a *word,*—which is, ONE of the moft COMMON in the ENGLISH language; and even denotes a perfon, exercifing an office,—which is of daily, and hourly ufe, to the *generality* of the world. Not to keep you longer in fufpence, —I muft inform, you,—it is,—the word,— SERVANT.

Now,

. Now, Sir, becaufe, it is the *duty* of the
KING, a MAGISTRATE, &c. to *do good*,
or, to *render fervice* to the *people*, who
are *intrufted* to *their care; therefore*, you
and your friends maintain,—that, *they* are
the SERVANTS of the *people*.

I muft confefs, that for fome time, I
thought,—this expreffion, was intended, only,
as an *harmlefs pun;* by which, you might
hope to roufe your readers, from any inclination to fleep, or propenfity to drow-
finefs; or by which, you might expeét to
relieve them from fatigue, or even perhaps, to foften their features, into a fmile.
But, however true it may poffibly be,—that
it has produced BOTH of thofe effeéts, upon
fome of them; yet,—that no fuch confequence, was *intended* by *you*, I am *now
perfeétly convinced*,—from the moft accurate
attention, to the uniform gravity, and conftant folemnity of your diétion. For, even
when you tell us, that KINGS are the *ob-*
jeéts

jects of *your laughter;* your words have not the leaft tendency, to move a fingle mufcle, in the face of any other man; except, it fhould chance to be, *at,*—and not, *with* YOU.

I muft beg leave therefore, juft to obferve, that however, *I might* be inclined to concur with you, in a *ferious* application, of the *term,*—SERVANT, to the KING, *could* it be CONFINED to *his office fingly,* without being extended to others;—yet, I muft confefs, I feel fome reluctance, to the adoption of fuch an application of it; becaufe, men are fo prone to err, that fome of them, would then perhaps imagine that it may with *equal,* or even *ftill greater* propriety, be applied, both, to YOU, and ME. And though, for my own part, I am totally indifferent, as to *any diminution of refpect,* which might chance to be the *confequence,* of fuch an application to *myfelf;*—yet, I fhould be extremely forry, on

on *your* account; if, any, of *your own*
congregation, fhould treat you with only
half the contempt, by confidering *you*, as
THEIR SERVANT; that YOU do a *king*,—
by confidering HIM, as YOURS.

Befides, if this were to be the cafe, the
very nature of the *relation*, between you,
and your flock, would moft unfortunately,
be totally reverfed. For then, it would
be *their office* to *teach*, and *yours* to *learn*.
It would be *their duty* to *preach*, and *yours*
to *hear*. It would then, be *their* RIGHT
to *iffue out their commands* to YOU, and
your DUTY to OBEY THEIR INSTRUC-
TIONS.

But, how difagreeable, and irkfome, *fuch*
a fituation muft *neceffarily* be to you; I can
eafily conceive, from that *noble freedom of
fpirit*, which breaths through *all* your writings; and which fo irrefragably proves,—
that you would fpurn with indignation, at
the

the *very idea*, of *submitting* to *any man's direction*, or even of *acknowledging*, any *man*, as your *superior*.

But, that such, would *soon* be the *horrible* state of *subjection*, to which you would be reduced, if your congregations, should *once* give the same appellation to *you*, which,—you do,—to the *king*,—is not merely a theoretical conjecture, but is a fact, which may be said to be sanctioned, by experience.

For, I know from the information, of some of the *ministers* of your *persuasion*, that this is the ACTUAL state of slavery, to which, *some* of *them*, have been already reduced: Of which, they complained to me; as a burden too grievous to be borne, and which therefore, they lamented as the heaviest of afflictions. Now, Sir, if the whole multitude of *Unitarian* congregations, should once universally *add* to their other enlightened tenet,

that

that *Jefus Chrift* is to be treated *only* as a *mere man*, this alfo,—that their *minifters* are to be treated *only* as *mere fervants ;*— how miferable then would be your condi- tion. And in the inftances, to which I allude, where, *fuch* has been the PRAC- TICE of fome congregations, they were certainly thofe, *who had embraced* the THEORY. For *they*, it feems, were juft as *incapable* as *you,*—of conceiving the *pal- pable difference*, and *diftinction*,—there is,— between,—the DOING ANOTHER A SER- VICE,—and,—the BEING HIS SERVANT. Hence therefore, they thought themfelves authorifed, to *compel their minifters*, (under the penalty of the lofs of their *wages)* to preach SUCH DOCTRINES, as the *richeft* and *greateft*, though not perhaps, the *wifeft* members of the congregation, fhould pleafe to COMMAND; and reftrained them from preaching *fuch*, as the MINISTERS, would *themfelves* have *chofen*.

I

" I will therefore beg leave, Sir, with all due deference, to submit, and leave the question, entirely to your own determination. viz. Whether,—as KINGS are *no more bound* to OBEY the COMMANDS of *their* SUBJECTS, than YOU ARE *those* of *your* AUDITORS;—it may not be,—in YOU, —*as just* and *as right*,—*as proper* and *as decent,*—*as humble* and *as rational,*—*not* to give the appellation of SERVANT, to a KING,—as,—it is in your CONGREGATION, —NOT to give it,—to YOU.

There are, Sir, likewise, some other passages, in *this* very letter of yours, to which, I am now paying my respects; which indisputably prove,—that had it been preceded by the manufacture of that very useful, but despised work,—a *dictionary,* it must necessarily have contained fewer apparent errors; and would have been of inestimable advantage to your *friends.* They being, I am persuaded, as much determin-

I i 2   ed

ed, *not* to *unlearn* any thing, which they fancy, they have been taught by *you;* as *you* can poffibly be refolved, not even to *examine* the *truth* of any pofition, which *you* imagine, *you* have *learned* from Mr. Locke. The *principle*, is the fame in *both;* though to be fure, the *authorities*, are *fomewhat different.*

For, you proceed to cenfure the expreffion, of—" Our Sovereicn Lord " the King," though only indeed, upon *political* principles. But, as fome of your *eleves* condemn it likewife, upon *religious* ones, I doubt not, but *you* alfo have the *fame* objeftion to it; though both, I am certain, highly venerate the title,—of— " the majesty of the people."

You are of opinion, that the *firft* term, if it ought to be ufed at all, fhould be applied to the *parliament.*

Now,

Now, if you mean by *this word*,—only,
—the HOUSES OF LORDS, and COMMONS;
had you but consulted some *Encyclopædia,*
which you must *necessarily* have done, upon
every *principle* of *book-making*, had you undertaken to manufacture a *new dictionary;*
—you would most probably, never have
urged this objection. For then, you must
have been uncommonly unfortunate indeed,
had you not learned from some one, or other
of them, that the *Lords* and *Commons*, are
only portions of the legiflature; but, that
the KING HIMSELF, also, forms, a con-
ftituent part of the legiflative body. That
every law therefore, requires *his assent*, as
much as the affents of the two houfes:
And his NEGATIVE, is as perfectly CON-
STITUTIONAL, for the REJECTION of an
act, as that, of a MAJORITY, in *either*
houfe. You would then also have known,
that, when we fpeak of the KING AS OUR
SOVEREIGN LORD; we do not, by that
expreffion characterife him, as a *part* of
the

the *legiflature*, but as POSSESSING *compleat-ly in himfelf*, the WHOLE EXECUTIVE POWER of the kingdom; and therefore, that ·IT IS A TITLE, to which, the PAR-LIAMENT, in *no fenfe*, in which, you can poffibly *take* that *word*, can have any more claim, than, even the *revolution fociety*; or, as Mr. Burke. calls it, the "*fociety for revo-* " *lutions.*"

By the ·*fame* means, you would moft probably have removed alfo, any *religious fcruples*, which *you* may entertain, as well as your difciples,—as to the propriety of the *fame* title.

For, no doubt, but you might then have gleaned up, at leaft, *fo much* acquaintance with *logic*, as would have imparted to you, *fome* knowledge of the *proper* ufe, and *fig-nification* of WORDS; and taught you, that the *very fame epithets*, *may*, by their appli-cation to *different fubjects*,—*receive*, from the

fubjects

fubjects themfelves, either, an *enlargement,* or *limitation* to their fignifications. Confequently therefore, though it would undoubtedly be blafphemy in us, to call the KING, OUR SOVEREIGN LORD GOD;—yet, it is certainly, not at all inconfiftent with *piety,* with *innocence,* and *good fenfe,* to call HIM, OUR SOVEREIGN LORD THE KING.

And indeed, where, even cuftom only, in a ftate had authorifed, or fanctioned *fuch* a *title;*—to withold it, is even to difobey an authority, which I hope you will pardon me for thinking;—though I differ from *you* in opinion,—*ftill greater,* than even *yours.* I mean, a learned ancient writer, called an Apoftle, notwithftanding *you,* have difcovered *his miftakes;*—who, has recommended to us,—I dare not, for fear of *offence,*—fay,—*enjoined us,*—" to " *pay cuftom, to whom cuftom is due, and* " *honour, to whom honour.*"

You

' You object indeed, I know, for, fo you have yourfelf told us,—to fuch 'titles, be- caufe, you think,—they are apt to inflate KINGS with PRIDE. But is not *this* a' *paf- fion*, which, it is as neceffary to be guard- ed againft,—for the fake of the peace, comfort, and happinefs of fociety,—in SUB- JECTS, *as* well as in KINGS. And will *you* then, that you may act confiftently, withold from *every* man, of any other rank, *his* title, from the fear, that the beftowing it, might excite the fame paffion in *him*.

Some men, for inftance, *may be proud* of the *title*,—of REVEREND DOCTOR,—how- ever it may have been *acquired*, or what- ever *right* they may *have* to it, or to whatever *rank*, they may be *entitled* to de- rive from it, in this kingdom; where al- moft every poor curate, has an unqueftion- able right to a rank, *fuperior* to numbers of thofe, who happen, to be *fo* dignified. But, were *he* to attempt to affume it, he
would

would foon be abafhed into humiliation, by the fupercilious brows of thofe, who, notwithftanding treat with *contempt*, the *ti-tles* of KINGS. Nay, though *you yourfelf*, may totally *difregard* the *recommendation* of the APOSTLE, give me leave to afk you, this queftion, whether, *even* YOU, Sir, would not have thought *me*,—if I had not ad-dreffed you,—*as*, THE REVEREND DOC-TOR PRIESTLEY,—to have been GUILTY, at *leaft*, of a BREACH of GOOD MAN-NERS.

From hence then, it clearly follows, that you yourfelf muft not only deem *that* man, if not ignorant of the rules, yet, however, to be deficient in the practice of good-breeding, who is fo tenacious of his own perfonal confequence, as to refufe to others, the titles and places, which are *really due* to them; *but him* alfo, who even refufes them to others,—from *courtefy*, which they ought

K k

not,

not, though they often do claim, as a
RIGHT.

I doubt not therefore, but that you
likewife think, that *good manners* are of
much more confequence, to the comfort of
individuals; and of much more importance
to fociety; than fome are apt to conceive; and confequently, that there are
claffes of people, who pay a much lefs
attention to it, as a part of *education*, than
it deferves. As it certainly tends, to ba-
nifh rudenefs and ferocioufnefs from fociety, and to produce the fame OUTWARD
ACTS of kindnefs, gentlenefs, and humility,
which chriftianity upon a different, and
better principle, enjoins. So that the hum-
bleft and beft *chriftian*, is in fact, the *beft
bred* gentleman.

Never therefore, I am certain, fhall
we difcover in future, any inclination
in you, and your friends, to with-
hold

hold from others, those titles, which, the *rites* and *customs* of a state, authorise any rank to assume. Since it is evident, that whoever feels *that inclination*, is actuated by the very *same* passion, which instigates the *possessors* of titles, to *pride* themselves upon them. Convinced, as you undoubtedly are, that whoever refuses to another, the appellation or the rank, which is due to him; can only be deemed as a counterpart to surly *Diogenes*, trampling, with *Cynic arrogance* upon the *carpets* of that *Plato*; who was as much superior to the *philosophers* of old, and also, of *this enlightened age*, in the *manners* of a gentleman; as,—in the brilliancy, and copiousness of his imagination;—the vivacity, and extent of his sagacity;—and the importance, and profundity of his discoveries.

As to that expression, which is so great a favourite with some philosophers, and undoubtedly, not less so with the vul-

gar,

ᴇᴀʀ, for it is to them, the title belongs,
—I mean, "ᴛʜᴇ ᴍᴀᴊᴇsᴛʏ ᴏꜰ ᴛʜᴇ ᴘᴇᴏ-
" ᴘʟᴇ;"—had you undertaken. the tafk, of
which I lament the want of execution;—
the explanation of this term, would foon
have been very eafy to you; and you
would, I doubt not, readily have feen, the
abfurdity and contradiction, which, it involves. For, though I do not think, that
any dictionary-maker, has *yet* been fo *enlightened*, as to join thefe words together,
as a *well-known title*; or even quoted any
paffage, from any *enlightened* writer, to au-
thorife fuch a junction; yet, to have difcovered the beautiful ᴀɴᴛɪᴛʜᴇsɪs, which
they form *both* in *fenfe* and *found*, there
would have been no occafion for you, to
have had recourfe to the ingenious *Cham-
bers*, nor the ftill more valuable *Scotch
Encyclopædia*, now publifhing; but, you
might have made the difcovery, from the
very firft fchool-boy's dictionary, you had

taken

taken up; if, his moiftened thumb, had
not torn off, or obliterated, the words.

For at what time, could this fame
much talked of MAJESTY, be breathed into
the people? Not furely, in a *ftate of nature,* when no government exifts,—but each
man is enjoying his NATURAL RIGHTS of
FREEDOM and EQUALITY, for the DE-
STRUCTION of each other? Was it then,
when no longer able to fupport, fo miferable a ftate of exiftence, they were feek-
ing to get rid of THEIR OWN SELF-DI-
RECTION, by fubmitting, to almoft *any* man,
who would take upon him the labour, of
GOVERNING them? Was it in either of
thefe fituations? If it were. However
glorious, fuch ftates may appear to modern philofophers, in thefe *enlightened times,*
THEY,—the PEOPLE,—evidently preferred
fubmiffion to a GOVERNOR, to *any* SUCH
MAJESTY. Experience, having foon taught
them, from THEIR OWN INCAPACITY,—for
fuch

such a choice; that it was much better to truft, to the feeming cafual fucceffion of nature, than to their own ignorant feleÂ£tion. Little dreaming I ween, at *that* time, that, they were thus furrendering up THEIR MAJESTY, of which, they had never heard.

Or was it, AFTER THEY HAD SUBMIT-TED, and were BOUND TO OBEY the WILL, or WILLS of others? If *this* be the TIME meant; had you, but taken the method I have propofed; and which I lament, did *not* occur to your thoughts; had you but looked out, only,—the words, *majefty*, *fovereignty*, *government*, *obedience*, and *fubjeÂ£ls*, you would have feen clearly, the abfurdity, and contradiÂ£tion, of fuch a phrafe. When therefore, you had heard, fuch an expreffion ufed, at the *revolution fociety;* your eye-brows, would fpontaneoufly have expreffed the contempt, you inwardly felt; and you would have been more difpofed,

had

had it been confiftent with *your good manners*, to have hiffed the perfons, who gave fuch nonfenfe for a toaft; than to applaud it, and drink it, perhaps,—" WITH " THREE TIMES THREE."

By this time I think, even YOU, Sir, muft fee *clearly*, how very neceffary it is, that men, fhould moft accurately examine, and moft precifely conceive the MEANING of WORDS; before they can pretend, to lay any claim to the character of REA-SONERS; or can form any pretence, to rank themfelves, in the number of WRI-TERS, SPEAKERS, or of CRITICS. From the want of this habit, which muft be the *fubftratum* of every *good* compofition,—it is, —that we may often hear a man fpeaking fluently for an hour, when to all the pur-pofes of inftruction, he has really been faying nothing; or read a folio, which though it coft the author, the labour of years to write, truly eftablifhes no other proof,

proof,—than this;—that the writer, *has proved nothing.* For, when by an accurate fcrutiny, into a fundamental propofition; we have once found, that the fpeaker, or the writer, had no clear conception of the terms, by which, it was compacted, and we have ourfelves difcovered, their true and proper fignification, we fhall fee the fpeech, or the book, at once lofe it's only principle of cohefion, and crumble into duft.

That you were not indeed *much fooner* aware of the neceffity for this practice, and did not moft feduloufly endeavour to cultivate it; I have the pleafure of thinking, was owing in no fault in me, but is wholly to be imputed, to your own neglect. For, *above twenty years* ago, I not only pointed *this,* out to you, but alfo, moft ferioufly advifed and intreated you, to give a clofe attention, to the *ftudy* of *every branch* of the *art* of LOGIC, not
indeed,

indeed, that you might improve, but that you might acquire a talent for ratiocination. And, the *more* clearly to *evince* to you, the extreme want, and abfolute neceffity you were under, of following this advice, I exhibited to you, the moft *direct*, and *ftongeft* proof;—by writing a little effay, entitled PRIESTLEY, *againft* PRIESTLEY, and fhowing, from your deficiency in thefe refpects, in *your effay upon government*, HOW YOU YOURSELF,—CONFUTED YOURSELF.

Upon this occafion indeed, a perfon who called himfelf *Eberacenfis*, threw down his gauntlet, and denied, that I had proved the charge. He certainly advanced to the combat, with much feeming fpirit, but with great real weaknefs; with a confidence, which nothing but ability, could have juftified, but with fuch powers, as only the moft bafhful modefty, could have fuited. The very

L l   firft

firſt onſet brought him breathleſs, and ſenſe-
leſs, to the ground; never more to riſe.
And I ſuppoſe, that by this time, at leaſt,
you recognize in me,—if you did not
before,—a certain writer,—who formerly
aſſumed, the name,—of *Ariſtarchus.*

But perhaps, you miſtook me for an enemy,
and therefore were reſolved, not to pay any
regard, to *my advice.* Should you however,
plead *this* as an excuſe, you muſt yourſelf
be ſenſible, that it can not by any means,
prove your juſtification. For, you can not
poſſibly, have ſo far forgotten the rudi-
ments of your education, as not to remember, that—*ſas eſt et ab hoſte doceri.* Your
conduct therefore, was as impolitic, as your
ſuppoſition was ill-founded. For, what poſ-
ſible advantage could accrue to any *enemy,* by *recommending* any thing, which, muſt
neceſſarily conduce to *your good;* and poſſibly, to his own injury. But with the moſt
                                  unfeigned

unfeigned truth, I can affure you; that if you *did really*, or *do now*, fo efteem me, you do me great injuftice, and are your-felf much miftaken. I can moft folemnly affirm, that there never was, *that man* ex-ifting in the world, for whom I ever en-tertained the leaft diflike, becaufe, we differed in opinion, or difagreed in fentiment. For, it is almoft impoffible to conceive, a greater contrariety of opinions, to fubfift between two men, who were both warmly attached, to the truth of chriftianity, than between me, and my late moft excellent friend,—Dr. John Jebb; whom I believe you well knew, and highly valued; yet, —we lived in the moft uninterrupted har-mony with each other,—from the com-mencement of our acquaintance in the univerfity, to the day of his death; though we never met without difputing, and by the account of his life, I find, we were once warmly engaged againft each other, in a

L l 2 *public*

public controverſy. Which, had I at *that time* known, ſhould have borne ſome marks of the ſincere affection, with which, I lov-ed the man, whatever might be the ear-neſtneſs, with which I attacked the argu-ments of the writer.

For, never ſhall I ceaſe to cheriſh the ſweet remembrance of him here,—and,—O! —that I may be deemed worthy to live with him, in eternal friendſhip hereafter. Many there were, who did injuſtice to his cha-racter, whilſt living, and who, now ſtill know not, one half of his real worth. For, he having early in life, imbibed ſome ſtrong prejudices on religious ſubjects,— his habits and connections, led him rather to cheriſh them; than afterwards, to em-ploy his own excellent underſtanding, in examining, and eradicating them. And, as his honeſt heart, was always warm in de-fence of the ſentiments which he embra-ced;

ced; he was fometimes led by his attach-
ment to others, to *appear to fome* as a
fiery zealot for his opinions; who in reality, would not defignedly have given a
moment's pain to any, the meaneft fenfi-
tive creature. For, no man ever poffeffed,
more " *of the milk of human kindnefs,*" and
never did I know, amongft *men*, (for I
muft mark that diftinction) a purer fpirit,
—wafted to heaven.—Pardon this digref-
fion, and permit me,—that,—

*His faltem accumulem donis, et fungar inani
Munere.*

But, Sir, from this pleafing,—fad remembrance, I muft once more turn my fteps,
to the thorny paths of controverfy; though
they will not at prefent be detained, but
for fome few minutes, longer.

Pardon me then, Sir, that if,—well knowing the " *rapid glances,*" you are wont to
take

take of books, I requeſt the favour of you, and can aſſure you, that *this requeſt* is made, as much for *your benefit*, as, *my own ;*—that,—when you do me the honour, of reading theſe letters,—you would be ſo good,—as moſt *attentively* to peruſe them,—TWICE at LEAST,—before, you undertake to anſwer them. Becauſe otherwiſe, moſt probably, your ſtatement of my opinion, will, through inattention, be a miſrepreſentation, and then inſtead of engaging with *me*, you will be fighting only with the air. For, as it is impoſſible for you, to *reply* to MY ARGUMENTS, if you have not allowed yourſelf, TIME ſufficient to *underſtand* them; and *ſuch* a *reply*, conſtitutes the very ESSENCE of all CONTROVERSY; YOU will be under the NECESSITY, of having recourſe to your moſt uſual mode, —of *calling* THAT an ANSWER,—which,— without even aiming, at a REFUTATION of your opponent's REASONING,—contains

merely,—

merely,—a RE-CAPITULATION, and RE-ASSERTION, of *your own opinions*. A mode of proceeding, which I can affure you, has fuch an effect upon fome *acute reafoners*, as to produce in them inftantly,—a *naufea*, at the very fight of any of your works.

Be fo good therefore, I befeech you, as to exert your own utmoft endeavours, and even call to your aid, all the affiftance you can procure, that inftead of taking the meaning of my terms for granted,—you may be enabled,—moft attentively to invef-tigate the *fignification* of *every word* I have ufed, in *every propofition*, which I have advanced; and inftead of contenting your-felf, with REPROBATING my CONCLUSIONS, WITHOUT PROOF OF THEIR being DESERV-ING of CENSURE, be pleafed with the *utmoft feverity* to *fcrutinife* the *chain* which *connects*, the CONCLUSIONS, WITH THEIR RESPECTIVE PREMISES. For, thefe are

the

the only effectual means, by which, you can either DESTROY my system, or that you can REBUILD *Mr. Locke's.*

It is to erect, or repair, a fit habitation for TRUTH, that is,—or ought to be, our primary object. And though she is then placed in a mansion most suitable to her dignity, when it is like those, which a *Plato* or a *Burke* has erected for her, ornamented with the finest polished marble pillars of the Corinthian order; yet, will she notwithstanding, sometimes deign to dwell in an humble cottage, supported merely by wooden pillars roughly hewn out of oak, and wrought only in rustic work.

That I might, the sooner, give you an opportunity of attempting to execute this work, so far at least as relates to CIVIL GOVERNMENT, well knowing how impatient you are, under any deprivation of labour;

bour; I have divided this correſpondence,
—into TWO PARTS; that you might not
be robbed of the pleaſure of returning an
anſwer, 'till *that time* was elapſed, which,
it would be requiſite for me, to employ in
writing the *ſecond* part.

I well know, with what agility and pleaſure, you always advance to the fight; and
with what tardineſs, and reluêtancy, you
retire. The nimbleneſs of the one, I have
been ſometimes induced to think, ſhows
more ſpirit, than policy. But the ſlowneſs
of the latter, can not be accuſed of want
of art; however, ſome may have ſuſpeêt-
ed it of the appearance of vanity. For,
often have we ſeen *you,* not only like
Antæus, as ſoon as you have been thrown
upon the earth, inſtantly rebound, with re-
newed ſtrength: But even,—when your ad-
verſary, has like another *Hercules, really
vanquiſhed* you, and ſuffered your *lifeleſs*
corpſe, to fall to the ground;—we have

M m   likewiſe

likewife feen you rife once more, re-anima-
ted with your former confidence;—and
when you knew the conqueror was certainly retired from the field, never more meaning to return;—we have heard you challenge
him again to the combat, fing a triumphal
fong, and claim the wreath of victory,—as if
you were really the victor, not the van-
quifhed.

I am, Sir,

Your very humble Servant,

S. COOPER.

END OF THE FIRST PART.

ERRATA.

Page 2, l. 12, between the words, *to* and *even*, infert '*almoft*.'
Page 18, l. 4, in the note, infert, between *when* and *they*, '*even*.'

Shortly will be publiſhed, by the ſame Author.

An INTRODUCTION to the STUDY of the
NEW TESTAMENT, in which, amongſt ſeveral
other ſubjeĉts of Enquiry, the true diſtinĉtion
between the INTERNAL and EXTERNAL
EVIDENCES of Chriſtianity, is, (in oppoſition
to the opinions of ſome very eminent writers)
endeavoured to be more accurately explained
then it has hitherto been, and the PRINCIPLES
of Mr. Hume's Philoſophy, from which he
deduced his Arguments againſt MIRACLES as
proofs of a Divine Revelation, are ſhown to
be contrary to the firſt Principles of our Knowledge, as deduced from EXPERIENCE and
TESTIMONY.

———————

Publiſhed by the ſame Author.

I. The Neceſſity and Duty of the early In-
ſtruĉtion of Children, in the Chriſtian Religion,
evinced and enforced ;—Preached in the Pariſh
Church of Great Yarmouth, on Sunday, June
the 20th, 1790; For the Benefit of the Charity and Sunday Schools. Printed at the Requeſt
of the Repreſentatives in Parliament, for that
Burgh,

                                        II. The

II. The Confiftency of Man's, Free-Agency, with God's Fore-knowledge in the Government of the World, proved and illuftrated. In a Difcourfe;—Preached in the Parifh Church of Great Yarmouth, on Thurfday, April 23d, 1789; being the Day of General Thankfgiving, for his Majefty's Happy Recovery.

III. The One Great Argument for the truth of Chriftianity, from a fingle Prophecy, evinced, in a new Explanation of the Seventh Chapter of Ifaiah: and in a general Refutation of the Interpretations of former Commentators.

IV. Confolation to the Mourner, and Inftruction both to Youth aud Old Age, from the early Death of the Righteous. In Two Difcourfes;—occafioned by the Death of his eldeft Daughter, who had only juft entered into her Twentyfirft Year;—To which is fubjoined, an Appendix, containing her Character, and two Elegies on her Death. Preached at the Parifh Church of Great Yarmouth.

V. Erroneous Opinions concerning Providence refuted,—the true Notions ftated,—and illuftrated by the Events which have lately happened

to

of Subfcription to the Articles and Liturgy. By no Bigot to, nor againſt the Church of England.

XI. Explanations of different texts of Scriptures, in four Differtations; 1ft. On eternal Puniſhments.—2d. On Chriſt's curfing the Fig-Tree. 3d. On Miſtranflations.—4th. On Chriſt's Temptation;—in which, the Notions of a Vifion, and the perfonal Appearance of Satan, are refuted.

XII. A Letter to the Biſhop of Glouceſter;—in which his Lordſhip's DIVINE LEGATION is defended, both from the Mifapprehenfions of his Lordſhip's Friends, and Mifreprefentations of his Enemies.

XIII. Definitions and Axioms, relative to Charity, Charitable Inftitutions, and the Poor's Laws. In which, Houfes of Induftry were firft recommended to the Attention of the Public.

www.ingramcontent.com/pod-product-compliance
Lightning Source LLC
Chambersburg PA
CBHW060607030726
47498CB00005B/1586